SELF-EMPOWERMENT

101

RE-ENCHANTMENT WITH OUR OWN CAPACITY FOR EMPOWERING OTHERS AND OURSELVES

SECOND EDITION

ROSIE KUHN, PH.D.

THE PARADIGM SHIFTS PUBLISHING COMPANY

SECOND EDITION

Cover design by Ponder at www.ponderhome.com

Text design by Highby Associates at www.highby.com

Text Font: Times New Roman

Production and editing by Lynne Krop at The Write Well: editor@thewritewell.net or http://www.thewritewell.net

Sufi folktale from Central Asia, adapted by Amy Friedman and Jillian Gilliland that can be found at:*http://www.uexpress.com/tellmeastory/index.html?uc_full_date=20070401*

Library of Congress Control Number: 2007907500
Publisher: The Paradigm Shifts Publishing Company
Orcas Island, Washington
ISBN 978-0-9835522-1-5

This book is dedicated to the donkey smugglers of the world

(See the story of Nasreddin as you finish this book.)

Table of Contents

Preface

While considering crossing the Atlantic Ocean on a 93-foot schooner, I knew without a doubt that I would most likely die. Why would anyone in their right mind choose such an adventure if they really thought they were going to die? Did I have a death wish? Was I tempting fate or was there something else stirring in me that would have made me decide to act in faith? At the time, I looked at the evidence of all the people who have crossed the Atlantic and figured the odds were in my favor, so I said, "What have I got to lose?"

I did not die, as fate would have it. In some ways, I was reborn. Something happened out there on the ocean that supported a leap of faith and out of that leap came a reinvention of my entire life. That moment was the beginning of the creation of this book *Self-Empowerment 101*.

I have created many wonderful and arduous adventures in my life; though, I saw myself as a reluctant adventurer. I would back myself into circumstances where I would have to go forward into an interesting, if not exciting experience or like deciding to cross the Atlantic, it took me many months to make the choice. My fellow sailors were on board with the idea from the get-go. I perceived myself as spineless, incapable of any real leadership or power, as through most of my life. Given the realities of living aboard a sailboat with six other individuals, I assumed I could hide behind the experience and competence of others. I didn't need any real authority or power and believed I would always be able to rely on others to give me the safety I needed.

The sailboat, *Tree of Life*, was my teacher and with her, I sailed to some very exotic places. It wasn't the destinations visited or the people with whom I sailed that made this journey exceptional. It was the relationship I developed with *Tree* that created an awakening. I had enough faith to agree to this voyage with the belief that if I survived, my spiritual self could only be strengthened.

During storms that seemed to happen only in the total darkness of the night, I felt frightened and distressed. I felt every wave roll under us and over us. Every moment felt as if this was the moment the sea was going to take me down into her depths and never let me up again. In every one of those moments, there was no doubt in my body or mind that I was going to die. I spent a great deal of time experiencing this overwhelming fear and yet, most often, it was only in my imagination that the possibility of dying truly existed.

In the midst of a large and rolling sea, with waves about 10 to 15 feet high, I came to find that if I lay in my bunk, on my belly, in the belly of *Tree*, I could feel her centeredness, spirit and connection with the cosmos. I could feel her agility and balance. I quieted myself down, became present in that moment to my senses and more aware of the presence of something larger and greater than I was. I was on a sailboat that was built to sail oceans. She was doing and being exactly what she was created to do and be. It was then only that it occurred to me that she, *Tree of Life*, was in complete union and harmony with the wind and sea. She was happy, in her element and having a magnificent time! Only then did I begin to feel her joy, spirit and love of the adventure she was born to weather. She was at home on the sea. I sensed all of this and in that moment, I surrendered my fear and heart to her. A sense of calm washed through me. In that instant, I felt embraced wondrously and secure within this vessel. I released my grip on my pillow and sheets, my fear and control and allowed myself to be rocked into sleep willingly. It was a moment of transformation.

The two-year experience aboard *Tree of Life* had a deep impact on me. I grew psychologically, spiritually, personally and professionally. I believe it is what led me to a Ph.D. program at The Institute of Transpersonal Psychology and to the San Francisco Bay Area. This is where my years teaching sailing, empowered me towards greater personal power and success far beyond any power and success I had considered for myself. It is what drew me to melding the transpersonal with transformation through workshops, retreats, coaching and writing; essentially, supporting people in developing deep spiritual and personal knowledge and wisdom.

Completing a Ph.D. does not necessarily give one a sense of competence to go out into the world and prosper, especially if that woman has yet to put herself out in the world in a way that is perceived as powerful and successful. In the Midwest, from where I come, it wasn't okay to be competent as a woman, except as a mother and wife. Pushing the edge of who I was becoming offended my mother and threatened my father. This was a time where a choice had to be made. Do I live a life that is acceptable to my parents or do I live a life that is extraordinary for me with side effects of setting precedents for my children and grandchildren?

Making a choice and living into that choice are two different things. By choosing the latter, I would say my life has never been easy, but it has certainly been rewarding. Striving to gain the approval of my parents, given their rules of conduct, would have meant an endless accruing of strategies to support their belief system. That would have taken me even further from my truth. As it was, I spent most of my first-four decades working toward that end. If truth be told, there is quite a few times when I diverged from the well-worn path and sought out what called to me, even though I often had little clue to where this would lead. Even now, I do not know where I will be taken during the journey of my life.

Like *Tree of Life*, being in complete union and harmony with wind and sea, I aspire to live in my element and love the adventure I was born to weather. I am at home on the sea of the unknown. Developing an ability to empower myself beyond the harbors of family and community, exercised and strengthened muscles that has led me to empower others. Each of us have this one lifetime within which to explore the edges of our soul and the capacity of our spirit to stretch into its vast completeness. I believe we are all equipped to live a meaningful and outrageous life; outrageously loving and having outrageous fun. My hope is that this book will support you to do just that.

Introduction: Being at Choice

Whether you are aware of it or not, you have a vision and you're bringing that vision into manifestation in this very moment. You may have a passionate idea, practice or business you want to bring into the world that has never been imagined in quite the way you imagine it right now. You believe in your idea. The question is, "Do you believe in yourself *enough* that you will deliver the goods, meeting your own expectations and those of the people you serve?"

No matter who you are or what you are up to, if you are starting an innovative endeavor of any kind—there are some fundamental issues that will confront you. These fundamental issues are big, scary and are elemental undercurrents running your life. As long as you are alive, issues of power, success and failure will be your constant companions. They will haunt you until you face specific beliefs, interpretations, judgments and assumptions you have made up about each of these concepts.

Your particular beliefs and interpretations either support or obstruct having what you say you want. The intention of *Self-Empowerment 101* is to support you in distinguishing and demystifying each of these concepts, diminishing their control over you and empowering you to be in a different and more fulfilling relationship with power, success and money than you may have ever thought possible. This will allow you to be at choice about how you *be* in your life in relation to personal power and success.

This book is not another how-to book; it goes much deeper than that. You have access to books on intentions, attracting what you want—books related to *The Secret* for example—and you have resources for financial success. This book takes you into the underworld of your thoughts: the residence of interpretations about yourself, the world you've created and that which you say you want. These interpretations residing in the deep recesses of your mind support your powerfulness and successfulness or they bring struggle and virtually kill your vision. If you aren't addressing these fundamental beliefs and interpretations, you are undermining your personal power and full potential for success, regardless of your intentions.

Some of us have a history permeated with experiences that point to our ability to create success and express personal power, as well as engage fully in our capacity for achieving whatever it is we say we want. Our personal history is filled also with experiences that point toward failure to live up to expectations, our own and those of other people. Where do you focus your attention when considering whether your enterprise is possible or impossible? Do you search the evidence you have for failure or for success? We are tested in our home and school environments throughout our childhood. Were you successful in the academic arena? What about in athletics? How did you fare when it came to dating and socializing? Who *were* you when you were with your friends?

You adapted your strategies to deal with so many different circumstances, in relation to the concept of power. How did you generate and use your personal power? What was it that supported your advancement through school? What support structures and resources were available to you then?

I wince when asking these questions because of the limited amount of success I experienced during my high school years. I had too many opportunities to see myself as a failure. I didn't have enough successes to provide myself with a sense of confidence and competence. A high school C- average did not reflect any great potential for success for this small town girl from Michigan. No one saw it coming—even I didn't—that I would end up with three Master's degrees and a Ph.D. Never underestimate the power of desire.

Any one of us stepping into fulfilling and prosperous work will need to engage with our issues of power and success. Why? Because we have developed strategic ways of being powerful and successful, based solely on our perceptions of power and success that we created in our past. We've been assessing what's right, wrong, good or bad about everything we think and do, based on beliefs we fashioned very early in our lives. The anxiety of these internal conversations send most of us back into hiding; deciding to play small and avoid potential failure and potential success. By recoiling into our comfort zones; however, we also avoid fulfilling our desires.

Whether you are a therapist, stockbroker, social worker, photographer, coach or consultant—anyone in the field of serving others, you train and educate yourself over years, spending thousands of dollars. Receiving your degrees and certifications, you then step into what you've envisioned yourself doing. Crossing this threshold marks the beginning of the phase of actually doing the work, taking the compulsory steps to have what you say you want; a wonderful and satisfying career. The fact is; thousands of people never step into this next phase. It's too scary!

Like a good coach, *Self-Empowerment 101* encourages *mindfulness* and a clear relationship to all the thoughts that come before the actions you are about to take. It is too easy to side step your amazing potential by avoiding a full investigation into which thoughts and beliefs are running your life, creating anxiety and denying you peace of mind and movement toward that which you say you want. You will uncover some juicy nuggets about your thinking process. I hope that the words on these pages will inspire you to remain curious and fascinated with how you decided to be *the you* that is embarking on this journey. My intention is to inspire you toward an expanded sense of personal power with far more potential for the kind of success you imagine.

Self-Empowerment 101 clarifies how your interpretations about success or power lead you to where you are exactly in this moment with your present circumstances just as they are. By choosing to avoid the investigation of your belief system and by avoiding choosing to distinguish what's valuable and what's not, you have done the same thing as choosing to be exactly where you are currently, right here and right now.

You have seen many people in your life repeat the same patterns over again, and creating one failure after another, while you stand back and ask, "Why the heck can't they see what they are doing?" You and I are just like them, in that we engage our lives without looking at the tools we are using to build our lives the way they are, with mistakes and failures, just like all those other people. We, like them, have limited vision because the lenses we wear were developed during our childhood. They are giving us a perspective that will limit us, no matter what. You may be the top CEO, the president of a country, a high school principal or a janitor; husband, housewife, man or woman; it doesn't matter. Each of you has a limiting set of interpretations that reduces your potential for further success. You have also the capacity to expand this limited perspective to include more clarity of vision, leading you toward a new and different practice that will indeed allow you to create that which you say you want.

Einstein said something like; we cannot solve problems using the same thinking that created them. It is our thinking only that leads us to limited success and failure. Individuals, groups and businesses with whom I have worked, and that have failed did so only because they were unwilling to look at, and shift their perceptions about themselves in relation to power and success. They limited their capacity to fulfill their dreams and undermine their potential by resisting different ways of looking at their world. It is our thinking that leads us to success. Successful people fulfill their dreams because they were not afraid to risk losing what they thought was theirs.

Risk is required in every moment. What makes it possible for you to get out of bed in the morning is that you have created an assumption that it is safe to get out of bed. You are willing to take the risk because you are willing to perceive the evidence that says this movement is safe. You have created millions of assumptions about what constitutes a risk and what does not. You are the sole decision maker regarding the leap of faith you will be taking today and across which chasm you will be leaping.

The intention of this book is to empower you to know and experience your true power and choose to live a successful life to the degree to which you want, no more and no less. Bringing mastery to your life and to your passions is extremely important in that, you need soul-nourishing experiences that bring about the fulfillment of your dreams. You need to experience everything it takes to manifest your desires. It is one thing to be given things by rich aunts or uncles. It's another to create those things through your determinations and your power. You never find out who you truly are, until you are willing to go for what you say you want. Everything is possible!

The focus of *Self-Empowerment 101* is on your relationship to the way you are *being* that generates the results you are getting. I believe your life can be fulfilling in an outrageous way by being in right-relationship to power and success. I propose that by reaching beyond your present level of perceived power, moving beyond your known strategies for getting by or getting through, you will begin a life-altering journey; a journey in which you will face yourself and all of your façades. It requires leaps of faith from what you know. You will tap into creativity most likely, and face some spiritual ideas that have gone unnoticed or unacknowledged before now.

What is labeled most often as *anxiety*, a sensation in your body that can get very uncomfortable, is one of the primal responses to life as a human being. It keeps you safe. It keeps you from doing things you shouldn't. It keeps you in the fold of what others want of you. That anxious feeling will arise when you think beyond the moment to include something scary. It will trigger a reaction, subtly or ferociously, to stop the discomfort. Anxiety can be a control freak in your life. It can become the master that you serve. No one likes to feel anxiety and so you do whatever it takes to make it go away. *The problem is that your dreams lie on the other side of these sensations.*

Some of you may be using most of your power to quiet the anxiety. Your capacity to be with anxiety, while taking the steps toward that which you say you want, will be a deciding factor in creating the success you want in all relationships of your creation.

Self-empowerment means we become more self-determining. We face emotions, thoughts, feelings and sensations, like anxiousness, that we empowered formerly to be bigger than us. We begin to take control and exercise muscles that will support us in limiting the interference of these thoughts, feelings and sensations. We feel the sense of power from the inside out because we master our own destiny, allowing us to live on purpose and face our fears more effortlessly.

Success

What is success? More importantly, what is success to you? It is paramount that you distinguish this concept for yourself. Only you will know whether you have met your criteria and your ideals successfully. Yalon, in the chapter "Relationship to (Im)possibility", is in the process of distinguishing his idea of success from other people's idea of success. He asks himself if he is striving to be a CEO of a major corporation because it fulfills his sense of purpose or because it's considered successful and fulfilling to other people. This is a crucial point for this high-level executive who wakes up in the morning not wanting to face another day at the office. Though he is making a huge amount of money and he has a great deal of status, there is something missing in his life and career. He wants to not only identify it, but also shift how he is being to either enhance his performance and sense of fulfillment in his current position or find a career that satisfies his need for true success defined by him only.

These are fundamental concerns in spiritual conversations as well. By denying and avoiding your true power, there is less opportunity to be engaged with God, Spirit, Source, Universal Oneness or any power greater than you. If you deny the importance of success, there is little opportunity for passion, fun and fulfilling your heart's desire. I believe that your calling—your purpose on this planet—is to fulfill your heart's desire. As you empower yourself to allow the fulfillment of those desires, you come ever-closer to fulfilling that for which you long, that in some ways seem unknowable until you are experiencing it. There is a profound awe in these moments that transform us. It is possible to bring these profound moments into your life on a daily basis, if you want.

It isn't up to me to decide for you what you want. I want this book to bring you an opportunity to choose your life and career from a place of true personal power instead of from beliefs and interpretations you have accrued over your lifetime. You can have what you want even if that means wanting to live unfulfilled and unsatisfied, then that is what you will continue to create. It is not a matter of being stuck. It is a matter of seeing how you choose to be stuck and seeing how it serves you to choose stuckness as a strategy. It's about you being willing to face potential failure while moving in the direction of potential success. Either way, your life will change.

This Book is for You

This book is for you if you have thought about seeing a life coach in support of creating your life and career. It's written by a life coach. The fact is, everyone stepping into their life's work faces the dilemma of deciding how successful, powerful, wealthy and healthy they want to become. You face questions regarding the degree to which you want to create, play and live on the cutting edge of your life. How willing are you to practice things that are hard or seem impossible in order to bring your ideas, dreams and desires to fruition?

Many events in history were considered impossible. It could not be done. Countless numbers of impossibilities are now occurrences we take for granted every day. What is it that the visionaries and inventors of the past, present and future have that allow them to create the impossible? Each of us has what it takes; I have no doubt about that. It's just a matter of doing what it takes. Are you willing to do whatever it takes?

A Book That Supports Your Coaching

The offerings in this book, in the form of exercises, practices, examples and didactic information are only part of a coaching relationship. A coach worth their weight will be someone who is your thinking partner, who is curious about who you are, beyond your circumstances and your words. Coaches want to know how you create your circumstances and how it serves you to create what you create. A great coach provides some teaching, some consulting, some handholding and a lot of space for you to empower yourself through your growth process. This includes taking responsibility for your creations; for being accountable to your agreements, others and yourself; for developing the muscles that support commitments, passion and inspiration and for untangling the underlying thought processes that are running all of the other programs.

Much like a computer, you have an operating system that keeps everything running and supports the software of current programs. It is important to look closely at what your operating system is delivering, what assumptions its creator made, what it expects and what it anticipates. A great coach, like a great computer consultant sits with you and inquires what it is you need and want from your system and empowers you to make changes to the operating system in order to allow access to many types of possibilities you don't know are available.

Sometimes we call in the experts to fix what's broken and that's good. Sometimes though, it's invaluable to recognize that you may be creating and utilizing strategies, intentionally or unintentionally, that cause the breakdown itself. Having a coach who can see beyond the present circumstances can empower you to shift how you are being and what you are doing to stop the breakdowns and/or be with the breakdowns in a more effective way.

The expert fixes things initially, but may get frustrated with you for not being accountable and responsible for fixing them yourself. Developing the confidence to fix your system, whether it is your thought system or any other system in need of repair, is essential.

Life coaching and business coaching are popular because everyone has a belief system, like the operating system on our computers that determines the level of success and prosperity that we potentially bring into our lives. We developed it over years of practicing being powerful and successful through the various means we've employed forever. The degree of success you have achieved so far doesn't matter. At some point, you will hit a wall that will prevent you from moving to the next level of success, fulfillment and confidence. Here's where your life can get really exciting! It is not the external circumstances that create the glass ceilings; it's your belief structure. Change your belief structure, take actions based on a new structure and allow yourself to expand into a more spacious way of being.

You may have noticed that the words be and being are *italicized.* One of the focuses of this book is you as a being and how you be this being. How you are being in your life affects everything that happens in your life. It is not what you do, but how you *be* while doing what you do. This may seem cockeyed at first, but as you read this book, you will begin to notice more effortlessly the state of your being and the choices you make because of how you are being. You will notice that a slight shift in how you are being can create a huge shift in what shows up in what you do and the results that follow.

This Book Reveals Another Secret

The Secret—in book and DVD format—is a huge success. *The Secret* speaks to the aspect of us who wants to manifest our dreams. As easy as it is to understand the dynamics of the Law of Attraction, understanding by itself will not manifest your dreams. It can't happen without participating actively in the process of your life. You want your dreams to come true with little or no effort and like most of us, whenever you hit a little bump of resistance, BOOM! You are off the track of that desire and onto something else; surmising that you can't have it or you can't do it. Something keeps getting in the way. As *The Secret* suggests; it's only your thinking that gets in the way. It is you only that creates the circumstances and experiences that are either in alignment with your dreams or not.

Engaging consciously in your relationship with power and success will enable you to reveal the interpretations that underlie your failure to get what you say you want. This will allow you to be with these interpretations of impossibility in a way that empowers you to make it possible.

The self-help field is a billion-dollar industry, but most people improve very little through self-help products. Books, tapes, CDs and workshops for self-improvement—how to become a millionaire is one example—are not going to make a difference until an individual's level of commitment to success is stronger than their commitment to safety, security and avoiding risk. There isn't a big secret in that! It is one's readiness to uncover those interpretations that block success and do something different that allows one's intentions to be fulfilled.

I know many people who watched *The Secret* and practiced the positive thinking suggested, yet they were frustrated with the lack of success that came their way. What needs to shift in order for them to create what they say they want?

Each Chapter Includes

Each chapter includes true stories about people who are successful in their own right, yet have had to shift some aspect of their being in order to create the personal power and success they want. There are exercises and practices—similar to those practiced by these individuals—for you to take on that will empower you to think differently and therefore, *be* different in your life; with the end result being that you are more at choice about how you are showing up in your personal and professional endeavors.

Most names are fictitious; however, Rick, Rick's wife Beth, Ko, Magi and Bree agreed to use their real names. They are grateful and honored to have empowered themselves to the degree in which they have and are happy to share parts of their stories with you openly.

Coaching Questions

Each chapter has a set of questions that a coach would ask you in relation to the subject at hand. Keep a notebook close by to record your answers to the questions. There are practices/exercises you can do as well. The more *you commit* yourself to the process and take action toward your intended desire, as with any book exercise that has the potential to empower you toward self-development, the more you will get from the experience.

Body-Centered Focus

Your body is a tremendous resource for true learning. Like your brain, every cell in your body stores information. This is part of our challenge with shifting our beliefs and interpretations because they are hardwired to our emotional and physical body that sometimes responds instantaneously to a mere thought. My experience as a teacher, facilitator and coach is that when individuals *get* something in the cells of their body, the learning is far more likely to stay with them than if they just get it in their heads.

This body-based approach allows an expansion of your capacity to *be with* the uncomfortable feelings of negativity and the more positive qualities. People are as uncomfortable with positive feeling as they are with negative feeling more often than you can imagine. What's that about?

We are *beings* in a physical form. The complex interweaving of our mind, body, emotions and spirit goes far beyond the intellect's capacity to articulate it rationally and logically. The poetic voice of the body speaks through sensations, informing us of a much larger, expanded capacity to know and experience this world. My intention is to empower you to be in a conscious relationship with the concepts of power and success and recruit the internal allies residing in your body that are far stronger and superior to your mind alone. It's not a competition, but an aligning of both the body and mind into a harmonious relationship, one that supports right-relationship with yourself and the world.

Originally, this book was part of a larger volume called *Becoming a Transformational Coach* that is close to completion and was designed for people who were interested in coaching, transformational coaching specifically. The intention of the following chapters is to engage the readers (e.g. new coaches planning to start a coaching practice) into thinking about what gets in their way of establishing a business or practice that is successful.

At the time, I realized as I was shaping this part of the book, that I was speaking to a larger audience, anyone who wanted to develop a practice, business, intimate relationship or a hobby, to a level of success that felt fulfilling and satisfying. This included financial endeavors, but more importantly, it embraced the nature of our being that wanted to know itself through creating and bringing things to fruition. It is essential for all to create a livelihood that sustains us financially and spiritually.

I believe that this book can shift you to *be* in right-relationship with your livelihood that will generate greater levels of self-empowerment, a greater level of fulfillment in many ways and a greater capacity for creating success in every domain of your life.

Writing Style

The type of writing used in *Self-Empowerment 101* brings awareness to the felt-sense or physical sensations of your being, located in your body. The information discussed in each chapter, when experienced through your body, will stimulate a physical reaction. It may be subtle, but *it is* there. By tuning into the qualities or felt-sense of these moments, you allow them to be acknowledged and explored. You have an opportunity to choose how you want to *be* with these qualities and sensations; perhaps desensitizing and demystifying them and reducing the fear and anxiety associated with them. By entering this process and by choice, you empower yourself to *be* more practiced and experienced with meeting any resistance that arises and can be present to it in such a way that allows resolution and movement toward what is next.

You will find that at times, the writing style may seem awkward and although the writing style is intentional, the awkwardness is not. My choice of words supports an ontological approach to coaching. *Ontology* is, in a nutshell, the science of the language of our being. How we speak and the words we choose, tell a great deal about how we think ourselves to *be*. So, if you think you are someone who is incompetent and undependable, it will show up very quickly in how you speak and write. My intention in this book is to write as accurately as I can to express what it is that I want you to get and understand. It will grow on you as you read.

What's in Store for You

Some say that nearly 80% of our manifested reality is generated from our subconscious. The chapters that follow explore this concept with the intention of creating a greater awareness of your thoughts and actions to be deliberate about increasing your ability to generate your life consciously or subconsciously, *being at choice* and *being responsible* for the life you create.

This book will explore power, success, money, confidence, accountability, responsibility, integrity and more.

Power

Power is always and everywhere. True power exists far beyond strategies, beyond manipulation, control and abuse. This chapter reveals the true power that is present already in you as you consider being fearless in the face of every circumstance that you encounter.

Success

Though we all say we are trying to become successful, so many of us limit and sabotage our personal and professional success unwittingly. We may have been working to be successful for years, yet never attended to how we are actually *being* with our work and our lives in a way that creates tension, anxiety, resistance or burnout. It's ironic that we work so hard to look as if we are being successful and then at the exact same time, we put the kibosh on our potential.

Money

People's relationship with money is a fascinating phenomenon and one of the most significant elements in their relationship to power and the achievement of success. Our beliefs, interpretations, assumptions and expectations about money are amazing in their capacity to influence and generate so much of what shows up in our lives. We emphasize money's importance and give it tremendous power to make us feel successful or make us feel like failures. We give it the power to make us happy or make us anxious, worried, depressed or diseased. In some cases, it has been given the power to kill; however, it is only the relationship with ourselves that influences our relationship with money. *It's not about the money!*

Confidence

When people say they lack self-confidence, what they lack is one, some or all of the components of confidence. Confidence is a conglomeration of qualities of being and when you sit still and truly feel confidence, you feel resourceful, experienced, knowledgeable, trusted, self-respecting and able to follow through. Confidence is not an all-or-nothing proposition. When feeling a lack of confidence, you are probably feeling that there is something missing. When we box all of these things up into one word, like confidence, it is so much more difficult to get a handle on just what it is that's missing. It's far easier to shift what we can see because it's just an aspect of confidence and only in degrees.

Accountability and Responsibility

This chapter distinguishes accountability from responsibility to investigate when and how you are being accountable for the agreements and circumstances in your life and to explore various ways to become more accountable to yourself and to your career. You will come to understand that your level of accountability reflects choices you made about yourself, other people and things, a long time ago. It reflects integrity as well and the degree to which you are in right-relationship with yourself.

Impossibility

If you believe that whatever you want is impossible to have, you will live a life settling for less than your full potential. You will live with regrets of *what if* and *if only* and you will avoid the potential of success by avoiding the potential of the agony and angst of failure. You will be consistent and vigilant about what you do and how you do it to keep yourself feeling secure and safe from any potential risk.

The intention of this chapter, "Relationship to (Im)possibility", is to provide you with an opportunity to choose differently about how you perceive what seems impossible. This is an extraordinary opportunity to *being* open and allowing yourself to have exactly what you say you want. This chapter opens the chasm between what you think is impossible and what you think is possible. There is a deep crevasse filled with the rubble of mistakes and perceived failures. We will step into the experience of failure to explore the components and the workings of this concept to demystify it and allow the potential for any of your impossibilities to become possibilities.

Choice Points for Transformation

There will be a moment, sometime while reading this book, when you will see that you are at a point of choice. You can choose to continue to see yourself at the mercy of your circumstances or choose to empower yourself toward transforming that which is causing you frustration and stress. Transformation can take place in a blink of an eye or over many years. It requires practice. It requires exercising muscles of self-determination, commitment, focus and follow-through. The difference between what I'm saying here and other books on power and success is that, here we are meeting the needs of a deeper process, one of distinguishing what your real sense of purpose is and your willingness to live into that.

My belief is that each one of us has unique gifts and talents. In order to bring these gifts and talents into manifestation, we are required to go through a metaphorical obstacle course made up of a menagerie of challenges and dilemmas that will strengthen our resolve and our mettle, empowering us to have what it takes. The degree to which you are willing to expand your capacity to be powerful through conscious practice in your life is the degree to which you will empower not only yourself, but also everyone with whom you come in contact. Enjoy the journey!

Chapter 1: Power

Our minds, our conditioning and our strategies are joined as we embark on the journey of self-empowerment. I would like to think that we are acting in the best interest of those we serve when we do what we do; however, too often, we do what we do because it serves us more than it serves others.

This doesn't have to mean something bad necessarily. When we act for our highest good, we act in everyone's highest good. The challenge is to distinguish between when we are acting from our highest good and when we are acting from our fears and our egoic desires. We can reveal the underlying personal power that motivates or inspires us to action by bringing this to light.

***COACHING QUESTIONS**: How are you using others to support your need for safety, security and invulnerability? If you are not using people, are you using their power?*

Power, like love, is infinite and everywhere. True power exists beyond and through the use of survival strategies. Through this chapter, you will reveal the potential for true power that is present already in you as you consider being powerful without fear in the face of any circumstance.

We encounter power, others and ours in every moment. It affects every cell in our body. By exploring and investigating your underlying beliefs, interpretations, assumptions and expectations about power, you begin revealing what may be stopping you from moving forward into the life you say you want. Through this exploration, you have an opportunity to identify aspects of your relationship to power that worked previously, but may no longer support you. At this time, you can create opportunities to be at choice with your interpretations regarding power and with the actions you take in relation to those interpretations. As you allow a different relationship with power to unfold and develop, you allow power and vulnerability to exist simultaneously.

Vulnerability—what's power got to do with vulnerability? You may be confronted with emotions, thoughts and feelings throughout this book that are associated with feeling vulnerable, weak and helpless. Perhaps memories of being victimized by someone's use of power over you will surface. There might have been times in your life when you were vulnerable to attack and abuse, so you learned many strategies for being invulnerable to other people's power. The dilemma is that, many of the strategies that kept you safe once can be ineffectual. You have a limited capacity to have the life and career you say you want, not because you are not smart enough or don't have the right resources and/or education; it is only the degree to which you are willing to be vulnerable in the face of what makes you feel vulnerable.

The use of power affects us, often creating sensations of vulnerability. It is my intention that through reading this book, you will discover a different interpretation of vulnerability, one that has you see you are now at choice when, where and how you are willing to risk yourself. Without the willingness to risk vulnerability, you may not move, access and utilize your personal power. Instead, you will use disempowering means to avoid intentional outcomes. In other words, you will choose to not to live directly into that which you say you want. You will take the safe course of action.

Are you willing to take the necessary steps to relinquish any obstacle related to power, including letting go of your beliefs about being vulnerable for the sake of following and fulfilling your dream? You don't have to decide now. I am confident that it's a choice you will make when you are ready.

I entered an internship in the field of marriage and family therapy during my late twenties when I first began developing my career. My supervisor saw that I was holding back and resisting my development in various ways. She asked me what that was about. I told her I was afraid that through my personal and professional development, I would become arrogant, self-centered and an unavailable know-it-all. I feared I would develop an inappropriate level of self-importance and I would abuse the power I had; I would end up hurting people. Throughout my life, I had observed many people using power in service for their own personal needs and consequently they hurt others as a by-product. I wasn't going to be one of those people who were vulnerable to the possibility of abusing power.

My career and my practice grew steadily, but slowly over the decades. Part of the slow growth came from my belief and interpretation about being powerful. I had no idea I could be powerful and still be in alignment with my integrity. My context for power did not include supporting movement toward leadership or success with kindness, compassion and strength. I worked slowly in order to maintain vigilance, avoiding vulnerability and the pitfalls of my interpretations of power.

COACHING QUESTIONS: *What pitfalls will show up if you step into your life powerfully? What are your beliefs and interpretations about being powerful that makes you play small? What are you avoiding in relation to power? With what are you vigilant in relation to power? Of what would you want to be mindful while fulfilling your desire for a great life?*

You will find that there will be times when you will want to avoid investigating your relationship with power as you read this book; however, the degree to which you align yourself with integrity and authentic being is the degree to which you will explore and reveal various motives for being powerful and for avoiding power. The degree to which you are willing to explore and reveal is the degree to which you will expand your capacity to empower yourself in becoming vital, creative and powerful. Are you ready and willing to take that on?

Avoiding the Conversation

Which part of you wants to avoid a conversation about power? Which part of you wants to avoid revealing your personal power by saying “I can’t do this; I need someone else to do it with me or for me,” or “I need a man/woman in my life to give me an identity and a sense of importance,” or “I’ll be credible only if I have an M.D., LL.B., Ph.D., CEO or MBA after my name." The belief that you require something you don’t have in order to have value and worth indicates a lack of *perceived* personal power. I don’t have it and I’m afraid that since I don’t have *it*, I will not be seen as powerful, important or sufficient. I will be vulnerable to mistakes, failure, rejection and humiliation.” The emphasis here is not on the *natural status* that you get along with your true interest in education or leadership, but for the *need* to give yourself an identity, worth and importance by believing you can get it from outside yourself. You will always be at the mercy of someone else’s perceptions of your identity.

One intention for creating a practice that supports self-empowerment is that you begin to rely less on what others think of you and more on your sense of worth, value and importance. It is fantasy that someone or something outside yourself can give you power and yet, history and myth support this fantasy. Just about every arena in your life requires you to have something to signify you have what it takes to be accepted, respected, hired, promoted, ordained, graduated or loved. If it looks like you are missing that which you think it takes to meet the standards, as most of us do, you will probably hide out and play small. It might not occur to you to look at what you have, instead of what you don't. Submerged beneath your strategies to get power through manipulation and control is a sincere wish to compensate for your sense of powerlessness, hopelessness and helplessness. You begin to believe you don't have what it takes to be powerful in a way that is in alignment with your true self. You could begin to allow your true authentic power to emerge by exploring and revealing the internal conversations you have about power.

This power is different from the power that comes from external sources. It is the power separate and distinct from control and that emanates from wealth, position and/or beauty. Control, dominance, manipulation and violence are not indicators of true personal power; in fact, they are actually symptoms of a perceived lack of personal power. They are forms of power over, as opposed to power that resides within and is expressed through your presence and through your being. Creating fear in others or controlling through manipulation and dominance masks your true nature in order to fulfill a need to remain invulnerable, survive or avoid threats and maintain security. These are all forms of power, but a challenge to understand and be with at first, maybe because you have developed all sorts of survival mechanisms to protect you from seeing and knowing about it. Hang in there! As you read on and as you work with the coaching questions throughout the book, it will reveal itself to you gently.

Stepping Into Personal Power

The work we have come here to do is to empower ourselves by individuating and self-actualizing. This means acting from your authentic foundation of personal power that comes through your self-expression and no one else's. This means revealing the, I should and the, I shouldn't of your life that doesn't belong to you, but to other people. You are in service to unconcealing your truth and core beliefs by practicing this reveal process. You may be out of alignment with your truth when you are acting from a set of beliefs that have you follow certain protocols. There are many religions, associations and institutions that have limited their capacity and your capacity for development and growth because the rules of the organization do not allow its own evolution to occur, nor do they allow individuals to express their unique beliefs and truths.

Each one of us is recovering, most likely from some form of oppression and the suppression of our unique individual expression because of our need to belong, fit in, be appropriate and conform to the norms of our families, religions and the societies within which we were brought up. Revealing how we stifled our personal power for the sake of being invulnerable to rejection allows us to be more at choice with how our lives can be different. Our relationships, world, the opportunities to individuate and self-express becomes less threatening and far more exciting and fulfilling to live in as we observe and witness how we are *being* in our lives.

COACHING QUESITONS: *At what point in your life did you decide that it was safer to go along with other people's plans and ideas? What strategies did you develop to hide your beliefs, desires, thoughts and ideas? Is there anything missing that, if it were present, would allow you to reconceal your true beliefs at this time? What would have to shift to support your acting according to your own truths?*

The Power We Give to Fear

We tend to be most effective in our relationships when we first reveal and acknowledge to ourselves our vulnerabilities, fears and need for power. We begin to demystify the power of our fears by doing so. We free ourselves from fearful thoughts, emotions and body sensations by shifting how we are *being* with our fears. We are then in service to aligning with our highest truth and our highest self, rather than aligning with our fears. We become far more compassionate and more spacious with others, their fears, their strategies and their own personal power.

COACHING QUESTIONS: *Focus for just a moment on a memory when you accessed the power that was inside you. What were the circumstances? How were you* being *in that moment that allowed you to access your personal power? What did it feel like in your body to be powerful from this internal source? Imagine what it would be like to live with the sole intention of living fully from this place of power.*

The power within you is the conduit of the wisdom and power always accessible. You begin to live, create and fulfill human needs and desires from a point of self-reliance, self-determination, self-mastery and self-actualization by recognizing and developing access to this power. It permits personal liberation from family, cultural, religious and societal rules and laws that include fear tactics often as a means to control and manage. You emancipate yourself from circumstances that are within your control and from what may appear to be beyond your control. You choose when and how you will be vulnerable, knowing that you have the wisdom and personal power to intervene on your own behalf if need be. You become the author of your life. You get to know what is true for you and what you have been afraid to know is true for you.

With this power comes the ability to exercise control, not over others, but over your thoughts, feelings and body sensations. Such a capacity allows you to assert your knowing, guiding your forces in a direction chosen by you only, despite consequences or outcome. This form of power lifts you to your highest potential, regardless of the odds, making what appears to be impossible, possible. There is no fear and no exploitation in true power and when you are acting from your personal power to support your highest truth, you are acting in alignment with everyone's highest good.

I'm not suggesting that you abandon your families, religions or communities. I am suggesting that you question your beliefs, how you came to believe them and whether these beliefs are in alignment with a deeper truth and knowing. This can be a disturbing process, but one that can lead to greater well-being for you, your family and your religious and spiritual community. It brings you to a moment of choosing which beliefs support your personal truth; a moment of discerning how to *be* in relation to others based on what is true for you.

The Paradox of Power

There are those who use ***power*** wisely and justly and there are those who do not. I know plenty of individuals who are afraid to be authentic in their power because of how they have come to interpret power. What has power come to mean? Power might mean yielding to the seduction of force, control, collusion, intimidation and/or authority. It might mean you could be judged as one of *them*. "It means being like my dad," says my client, Rachel.

There are many people who don't want to be like their parents because they saw their parent's abuse of power. Not just parents, but teachers, priests, politicians, friends, lovers, brothers and sisters; just about everyone they know abused their power in one-way or another. So, like Rachel, they decide to relinquish their own personal power for the sake of staying small, safe and harmless. This means they have given up being in a harmonious relationship with their personal power—the ability to know, speak and act upon what is true—for the sake of position and a felt-sense of security, which is just another form of power.

The trouble with talking about power is that we don't seem to comprehend that we are always power-*full*, even while sitting on the couch doing nothing and choosing to look and feel power-*less*. We exercise power when we choose to think particular thoughts and when we choose not to interrupt the thoughts we don't want to have. We use power when we tell the truth and we use power when we choose to withhold the truth. We use power when we act in alignment with our word and when we choose to procrastinate or do something else entirely. We are always being powerful. It just looks different from the power we witness in gold medal athletes, corporate CEO's, political leaders, actors or anyone we observe being powerful.

We cannot *not* exert power. As long as we live on this planet, we have the power to say yes or no. For many, living powerfully means brutalizing others, but it also means standing up for your beliefs at the risk of being brutalized for the right to have those beliefs. Throughout history, millions of people, for the sake of their beliefs, have taken up arms or thrown them down powerfully. They have gone to war and gone to jail. They have abandoned ships and abandoned their countries. The have aborted fetuses or they have protested the use of such measures. The have been hanged and spat upon, cursed and stabbed, raped and left to die because they had the power to do so.

People have also saved lives, created huge changes in the way we live and the way we see the world. They have created inventions, technologies, medicines and awareness's that go beyond what we once believed as impossible. Why? Because their beliefs were stronger than their fears. This is power in action.

Identifying Power through True Innovation

The exercise of true power can result in the development of amazing technologies that support the betterment of the world. Here are two examples of individuals who founded organizations, starting with a vision and a belief about what was possible. A more conscious world is emerging because of people like these who are willing to generate their lives from their personal power.

Victoria Hale

By creating the first nonprofit pharmaceutical company in the U.S., Victoria Hale is working to develop safe, effective and affordable drugs to treat neglected diseases that afflict largely more rural and poor populations in underdeveloped nations.

She grew up in Baltimore and worked as a pharmacist at the Johns Hopkins University Hospital. She earned a Ph.D. in pharmacology at the University of California, San Francisco and reviewed drug applications for the FDA, served as a senior scientist at Genentech, served as an adviser to the World Health Organization and cofounded a drug development consulting firm called Axiom Biomedical, Inc. A lifelong admirer of the early women's suffragists and of Margaret Sanger, she was one of six women scientists who fought to require pharmaceutical companies to include women and children in clinical trials. This dedicated group was responsible in some part for changing the way clinical trials are conducted in the industrialized world. She says she learned at that moment that, "a small number of committed people can make a lasting difference on an important issue."

Victoria began to rethink the profession she loved, by her late thirties, because she felt it had departed from the ideals of healing that drew her originally. During a trip to India, she witnessed the ravages of leishmaniasis and knew she had to do something about the epidemic. She returned determined to start what she had been told was impossible—a nonprofit pharmaceutical company that specialized in developing drugs for the diseases of the poor. In 2000, Victoria and her husband, Ahvie Herskowitz, a cardiologist, founded ***OneWorld Health***—a nonprofit pharmaceutical company—to bridge the gap between neglected and infectious diseases and pharmaceutical science. *OneWorld Health* develops safe, affordable and effective new medicines for people living with diseases of poverty in underdeveloped nations. *OneWorld Health* seeks to bring much-needed drugs to the market for a fraction of the usual costs.

OneWorld Health demonstrates that it is possible to develop new medicines for neglected diseases of poverty using an entrepreneurial, nonprofit model. The *OneWorld Health* nonprofit pharmaceutical model brings together experienced and dedicated teams of pharmaceutical scientists, identifies the most promising drug candidates and develops them into safe, effective and affordable medicines through extensive clinical trials.

Victoria Hale challenged the assumption that pharmaceutical research and development is too expensive to create the new medicines that developing nations need so desperately. Victoria, with *OneWorld Health* maintains her vision to develop affordable, effective and appropriate new medicines for the poorest of the poor where they are needed most.

Aresa

Aresa is a development company with plant biotechnology. It was founded in 2001 by Carsten Meier who is the present Chief Scientific Officer. Aresa has its scientific outset from the Institute of Molecular Biology and Physiology at Copenhagen University who have supported the company since its foundation with consulting, facilities and scientific staff.

RedDetect – Plant for Land Mine Detection

Aresa developed a BioSensor for detection of land mines and unexploded ordnance devices on agricultural land. The BioSensor is a genetically modified grass-like plant that can sense nitrogen dioxide in soil and changes color from green to red when growing in or near proximity to land mines.

Many thousands of innocent people in countries such as Croatia, Vietnam and various parts of the Middle East and Africa are killed every year by unexploded land mines and other non-detonated devices. This innovative product developed by Aresa will impact the safety and well-being of people all over the globe powerfully.

The Consequences of Owning Power

There are consequences of owning power. Each of us has a set of perceived consequences for living from within this personal power. "I will lose my inheritance." "My father will throw me out of the house." "I will lose my job." "I will lose everything." I will look like a geek." "My wife will leave me." "I won't be popular." "I won't get laid." "I will lose my identity and become like a woman who *needs* a man." "I will lose the sense of safety I have built around me." What this means is, if you live from your personal power, you will have to give up the perceived security of your present circumstances, regardless of whether they are fulfilling or not and you will have to become responsible for your own happiness, fulfillment and well-being. How many people do *you* know who really want that?

How We Developed Our Interpretations of Power

Consider that as very young children, each of us decided what was real based on observing our external environment; this included watching friends and neighbors, teachers and our parents being themselves. Based on what we saw, heard and imagined, we created a theory about the world and lived into the theory as if it was the only reality. This is power in action, don't you think? That as small children, even as infants, we have the power to create a reality based on what we observe and experience. An interesting note here is, if you look at the theories of personality presented by the most well known psychologists such as Freud, Piaget, Skinner and Jung, you will find that each of their theories is based on the experience and beliefs created by that individual's childhood. Their personal experience gave them a frame of reference from which they shaped a world-view. This view of their world shaped the world of anyone studying, practicing or receiving psychological support. Our childhood beliefs and interpretations affect every person with whom we come in contact throughout our lives.

Individuals with brothers and/or sisters may have noticed that each one of their siblings created their own personal reality through interpreting mom and dad's needs. Each child created a unique and personal strategy based on what they saw, heard and imagined. Each used power to mask pain, isolate or be humorous in sad, anxious or frightening situations. They used their power to be good while others are acting mean and abusive; stayed quiet when they knew they had something to say or pushed back, even though they knew it might cause them harmful consequences. There are also those children who use personal power to achieve and be successful. Sports, arts and academics are some of the arenas within which children use their power and achieve a healthy relationship with power.

Being powerful in dysfunctional families often means intimidating, manipulating and abusing ourselves and others to get what we want. I watched each of my eight siblings and I get theirs and my needs and desires satisfied, sometimes in very heartless ways. Intimidated by bullying brothers and fighting sisters, I decided early on that I could be most powerful in my family by being nice, good, pretty, quiet and undemanding. If I wanted anything, being meek and non-threatening was more likely the way to get it, if I were to get what I wanted at all.

I used my power to avoid personal disappointment, *rejection, hopelessness* and *powerlessness* by satisfying other people's needs and wants. This was much safer and I was far less vulnerable to attack. I believed, as long as I met other people's needs, I would be loved, appreciated and acknowledged and I would never be abandoned or rejected. I pretended I didn't want anything and after a while, the pretense became reality. What a great foundation for a therapist, spiritual guide and life coach!

We adapt ourselves psychologically, as young children, to our circumstances. We observe and notice the world around us and begin functioning in ways that ensure our most basic needs of being nourished and nurtured are met. We develop specific strategies that become foundational patterns of *being*. We come to believe that by fitting into the environment created by our family and by our culture, we can avoid rejection and/or abandonment and continue to feel as though we belong and are loved. There are thousands of children for whom this approach doesn't work. Regardless of their desires and strategies, they cannot get their foundational needs met. The results can include death, violence and/or mental illness.

Just as driving a car becomes automatic over years of practice, *functional* or *dysfunctional* strategies for survival become so ingrained in our consciousness that they actually convert to subconscious responses. We come to identify ourselves with these strategies and they form aspects of our personalities. These patterns of *being* and behaving give us a sense of power over our circumstances, but over time, they strip us of our personal truth and the use of true power.

COACHING QUESTIONS: *What did you decide was the safest way to operate in your family? How did you use your power to get what you wanted? What tools and strategies did you develop to survive the misuse of power in your childhood, at home, in school and with friends? In what ways are you using the same tools and strategies today? What would shift if you found new ways to be with your personal power? What is possible from this new way of being?*

Power of the Beloved

I believe the power that generates everything on this planet and in the Universe is the Universal Source of Life. In the spiritual vernacular, it is the Beloved, the One, and God. If this is so and if we are all powerful beyond measure, then in what ways do we want to use this vast resource of power?

I believe we have innumerable choices; however, most of us make our choices based on how we need to *be* in order to survive. We make interpretations based on our circumstances. We make interpretations and then use our power to create strategies to support those interpretations. Until we reveal and acknowledge these interpretations of power, our behaviors and our way of *being* with our environment will continue to be controlled by something other than our true self. These interpretations create a holding pattern that may keep us feeling safe, but does not support attaining our dreams and desires for a powerful and fulfilling life and career. We just continue to suffer, settle and survive.

Think of a helicopter. It has the capacity to use its power to move up, down, forward, backward and side-to-side. It can virtually stand still in mid-air in what appears to be a static position. It is using the same amount of power and energy to stay in that holding pattern as it does to move in every other direction. Staying in a static position is how many of us use our power; existing within the same patterns, even though we have the capacity to move in any direction we want. It takes a lot of power to maintain a holding pattern, resisting the forces available to support us in moving in any direction we want to go.

Power to Change Our External Environment

Most of us use power—other people's power and our own power—in the effort to change our external environment, including people and circumstances. We use various forms of manipulation and control as strategies to ensure we maintain a sense of control within our world and sometimes over our world. This provides a perceived sense of security and stability; however, these strategies come from a belief based on fear and this fear comes from perceptions we created in our childhood. I have heard clients say numerous times, "If I don't control my environment—my family, partner, bosses, employees, etc.—I will lose my sense of security. When I imagine this, I feel helpless and powerless. I don't want to feel this way. I would rather keep things the way they are than face the fear of losing everything." These clients are in a stalemate with themselves. They have hopes and dreams to fulfill, but their drive for fulfilling their aspirations is extinguished by their fear of the consequences, their perceived loss of power and control, safety and security.

True power is not about controlling our external circumstances or environment. It's not about having all the right accoutrements. It's about establishing right-relationships with oneself. Being in right-relationship means acknowledging the internal generator of your personal power, practicing trust in your own truth, being respectful and honoring of this truth beyond what appears to be true in our external environment.

As long as we play in the safe arena of security and not in the arena of personal power, we impede our own capacity for personal power and continue to act in ways that diminish our fullest creative expression of personal power.

It is my intention for you to reveal, recognize and acknowledge first your internal environment from which you access your personal power. Being powerful is effortless and allows you to speak what is yours to speak and do what is your to do from this place. You then have an expanded capacity to *be* with others and their expression of personal power.

COACHING QUESTIONS: *What are you afraid people will decide or find out about you as a powerful person? What do you do so people don't find that out? How is it working for you to use these particular strategies? If you let go of the fears of what people may find out or decide about you as a powerful person and let go of the strategies associated with those fears; what will show up?*

Life Just Is … Circumstances Don't Just Happen

Circumstances are vehicles through which we express ourselves. There are circumstances we generate, create or gravitate to because they allow us to feel most like ourselves and there are circumstances we avoid because we don't like to experience ourselves in ways that feel uncomfortable. Generating, creating, avoiding and denying are each a strategic use of power to get what we want, whether that be safety and security or cutting-edge changes in our lives within our given circumstances.

Seeing yourself outside your current circumstances is a challenging practice, but if you can do it, you can begin to use your power to move beyond what you think is true—in relation to your circumstances—in order to create a different way of being. Life is just life. It's how you choose to *be* with life that makes the difference. Gurus and spiritual teachers talk about this all the time. You get to decide how you want to *be* with your life, circumstances, beliefs, thoughts, emotions and allow yourself to know what you want and deciding how you want to be in relation to that is a significant and self-empowering practice that can be extremely profound. This is an ongoing life practice. Layers upon layers of truth reside within each of us and through curiosity and fascination, each of us has tremendous opportunity to be surprised by our capacity to grow and generate amazing things through our personal power.

The test of true power is being who you are in the midst of any circumstance, maintaining connection to your ground of being and your internal source of self. From this place, regardless of your circumstance, you can move into your work with integrity, dignity, clarity and grace. There is no reason to defend, resist or control if your true desire is to maintain a healthy connection with yourself and the circumstance within which you are being.

COACHING QUESTIONS: *What stops you from knowing what you want? What stops you from having what you say you want? If you were to look at what stops you from having what you say you want and the actions you are taking to support that, to what would say you are committed. How does this influence the choices you make in relation to what you say you want?*

Power and Work

There are many aspects to creating a life that scares us into playing small or hiding out in jobs and relationships that are anything, but nourishing or nurturing. For example, I would say, marketing and selling are two aspects of career development that can wipe out a majority of entrepreneurs. Having to speak about their gifts, talents, expertise—in essence their personal power—shuts them down. It is too frightening for them to reveal or expose themselves. They feel too vulnerable when sharing with others what they want to bring to the world. It goes against all that has been entrenched in their psyches about not tooting their own horn, not being boastful or arrogant and/or not showing off. We learned to play small because of how we grew up. It challenges our belief system, on a cellular level, to act contrary to our early learning, even when that learning interferes with moving toward the success we say we want.

We tend to use our power to prevent feelings of discomfort, fear and anxiety from occurring. We also use our power to deflect potential responses from others (e.g. rejection, ridicule, failure, as well as attraction, appreciation and love). I add the last three examples because many of us are as challenged by being attractive and successful as we are with rejection, ridicule and failure. We use our power in any way that will keep us within our comfort zone.

Role Models for Power

Every person who comes into your life is a role model for power. Of whom do you think when you think of power? Do you think of government leaders, parents, or teachers you had in school: your boss, colleagues, spouse or friends and brothers or sisters? We have plenty of models of power who display effectiveness in controlling by fear and intimidation, but is this really an effective strategy in leading teaching, connecting or relating? We have politicians, teachers and all types of individuals who abuse their power and the people they say they serve. This I believe, is our strongest interpretation of power and based on this interpretation, too many of us avoid being powerful in the truest sense of the word.

My dad was a role model of power for me. I wonder now about how secure he felt with himself, since he rarely allowed others to voice their own opinions and truths. It was his way or the highway. I grew up frightened of having an opinion. I learned to want what he wanted. I dismantled my own truth for the sake of exercising ways of being that followed his belief system. During my adolescence, because of the interpretations I created about myself in the world where I lived, I felt powerless. I was unable to generate acceptance from him and it did not generate self-acceptance either, regardless of how I was being. The experience of not knowing how to be me was debilitating and despairing. I had to reach out for help from therapists to become clear about who I was inside the façade.

I have done my share of controlling and manipulating. Like my father, I became an expert at showing up in ways that made people feel bad about them so I could feel good about myself; however, over time, I experienced many people who actually allowed their personal power to shine in healthy ways. They modeled the power of allowing the true essence of self to come through. How inspiring! How illuminating to witness a form of power in another that actually allows each of us to shine. I've been touched deeply by these teachers and in turn, I want to teach in kind.

I want to model what this form of personal power looks like because I facilitate coaching training programs grounded in integrity and accountability. I have to practice walking my talk. I need to practice stepping onto the edge, heart open and ready to expand into my truth and the power that emanates from within. This power is just another window through which I look, in order to find myself again and yet, in a different form.

Initially, it may feel uncomfortable when you reveal and recognize your own use of power to manipulate people and circumstances. By acknowledging how you've been *being*, you actually empower yourself to be more at choice in how you can relate differently and be more accountable to yourself and those with whom you associate.

Issues with Power

Like each of us, my clients and students have issues with power. They call it something else, like relationship issues, sexual issues, money problems, health challenges, spiritual dilemmas, difficulties with their mother and issues with their postal person, but all of it comes down to this one word—**POWER.**

We use our power to experience illness and accidents. We use our power to play small and become victims. We use power in countless ways that look more like disempowerment and feel un-power-full. We make believe we are weak and helpless to support the interpretations we created earlier in our lives.

It's extremely important to reframe what feels like disempowerment into a misuse of power so that you can see how you are creating or maintaining the circumstances that are not fulfilling or satisfying and may be hurtful to you. You may be using your power in a way that does not serve you or anyone else. It may be serving a belief structure that does not support or empower you.

NOTE: I encourage you to reach out and get help immediately if you are experiencing self-abuse or abuse from others. This can be the most empowering thing you ever do in your entire life.

Using Power to Stay Small

This is a recounting of a client's unveiling of her disempowering use of power. In this account, you will witness the use of power in order to stay small. It isn't very pretty and you won't necessarily like what you read, but it is a wonderful example of what so many of us do without conscious consideration of the consequences we create unintentionally.

Melanie, a brilliant, amazing and creative woman, designs her life around men who use her and treat her as a second-class citizen, and why? She believes she needs a man in her life to give her an identity, to give her status and to her, this means power. Melanie believes she does not have what it takes, the personal power to create a successful career or identity. She insists on using other people's power to get her what she says she wants.

Melanie is an East Coast woman with an MBA. She has an entrepreneur's spirit and enough energy to bowl over anyone who stands in her way. She comes also from a military family, wherein, she decided she was destined to become a General's wife. The man she married was on the path toward being a high-ranking officer, but detoured instead toward academics and a Ph.D. at Yale. Her chosen career path was okay with her husband. She could see herself as the wife of a tenured professor at a major university. As it turned out, her husband never finished his Ph.D. program, never got that position with a university and Melanie never got that identity for herself she had designed.

With the demolition of her dream of success through her husband, Melanie has resisted being the breadwinner of her family, for the greater part of her thirty-five year marriage. She avoided this position in order to maintain her vision of someday having the man of her dreams provide the life of her dreams. While doing everything she could to encourage and cajole her husband to step into a career of any sort, she was deflated constantly with the lack of enthusiasm he displayed while appearing to search for a job. As they both approach their late fifties, it becomes more obvious to Melanie that she cannot get her identity needs met through her husband. Both look disempowered and yet both have taken a very powerful stand to look helpless, hopeless and powerless.

At this time, as in other times in her life, Melanie has used the services of another man to fulfill her requirements for identity and power. She has gone into business with a brilliant and well-educated businessman who, in his early fifties, has yet to be successful at what to what he seemed destined. Like Melanie's husband, he too has dodged employment powerfully. He's been unable to get the right breaks or the right deals to get his career off the ground. He relies continuously on the support of others while he sojourns toward his destiny of success. Melanie believed this man would give her the corporate identity she has needed to be successful in her career. In the four years they have been working together, they have made very few inroads into a successful business practice. Their commitment to success is mired by their use of power to destroy any evidence of success that begins to come their way. They spend exhaustive amounts of time arguing and defending their individual tactics for approaching clients. They have priced themselves out of the ballpark and they can never close a deal or maintain clients. On top of that, they choose not to get support from consultants or coaches.

I find it very fascinating that all three individuals, who are brilliant and have amazing potential, do not move ahead. They are using their power to resist and avoid something. What the heck could that be?

Melanie is beginning to see, through weekly coaching sessions, how she uses power to manipulate, control and victimize herself and her partners. She has a story about herself and how she needs to be rescued by a charming, but ineffectual man who uses his power to avoid his personal success, whatever that means to him. In turn, Melanie becomes the rescuer and a disenchanted heroine. She lives on hope that *someday* things will turn around and these men will begin to produce the promised conclusion to her fantasy. It hasn't happened for her in her thirty-five year marriage, nor has it happened in her business partner's life. Her commitment is to remain in the illusion of needing to be rescued, but the spell is wearing off.

My job, as Melanie's coach, is to reflect the reality of what she presents week after week, in order for her to see how she uses her power against her own ability to create amazing accomplishments and all on her own. She has empowered her belief in wanting to be a femme-fatale, helpless and vulnerable. Melanie is just moments away from conceding that she has been creating a smoke screen in order to avoid her personal greatness for the sake of staying in line with a cultural norm and myth about what a real woman should be.

Like Melanie, many of us give away our power in powerful ways for the sake of maintaining our belief that, living within the cultural norm is a safe place. We believe that relying on the power of others—including our families, culture, religion and government—we will get a fulfilling and satisfying life; a promised life. These institutions rarely, if ever fulfill their promises.

Changing Disempower to Power

It takes a great deal of practice to find our way to the power that serves our highest truth. It has taken most of my life to understand that being powerful means quite the opposite of the power with which I was raised. It has taken decades to speak aloud that I am powerful, without wincing, ducking or running for cover.

Imagine for a moment the power that comes with the idea of rank and privilege, the power of playing the victim, the power of being the hero and the power of religion. What about the power of beauty, wealth and sex? Each of us strive for this kind of power, being human after all, but now imagine the power of being self-actualized, the power of accountability, the power of love, the power of dignity, integrity, humility, failure, the power of owning what is true, the power of stepping into that truth one moment at a time. Can you feel a difference?

COACHING QUESTIONS: *What would you have to give up to live honestly from your personal power? What would it be like to live without that? Are you willing to try it for a week just to see what shows up?*

Bruce Lipton, in *The Biology of Belief,* explores the phenomenon of thought as the driver of cellular functioning. He found, through years of research, that DNA is not the designer of our destiny, as we had believed once. Now it appears with remarkable certainty that it is the cell wall of each cell that is the brain of the operation. The cell walls have the same chemical structure as a computer chip and exactly like a computer chip; they receive input through the energy exchange based on perceptions. The power of our beliefs determine our biology and our destiny. This is just one of many examples of how we are able to access our internal and eternal wisdom any time we want. True power is the utilization of this wisdom for our highest good.

Putting Power to Work: Practice Areas

In creating a practice, you are presenting yourself with an opportunity to investigate your relationship with your power and the way in which it is used. This is also an opportunity to notice your fears in relation to yourself and others. It's an opportunity to notice where you give your power away to others for the sake of safety, security, looking good and for the sake of avoiding having something taken away from you. Here are some practice areas that will support you in revealing your use of personal power.

Before you begin, I encourage you to write down what it is you say you want and the outcome you say you want from this book, this chapter and this set of practice areas. With this in mind, you can track what's working and what isn't. Some people set up a spreadsheet or other tracking mechanism to support their practice and accountability. You will see that in each chapter, I encourage you to get support from a coach, therapist or any other person you feel has the capacity to empower you and keep you accountable to your word. Decide how you will gauge the gains you are making through the coaching questions and practice areas. What structures do you want to create? What time line would work for you? I am encouraging you to find what works for you. If it doesn't work, find a different way to work or perhaps just decide that what you want doesn't matter enough to do the work. Just let go of doing the practice areas and see what happens.

Practice Areas

- Notice the events and circumstances within which you exert power or control.
- Notice any underlying conversations that have you shrink from your personal power.
- Write down beliefs you have about yourself, others or the world, that have you exerting control, manipulation or exploitation (e.g. they need me to take care of the situation).
- Ask yourself, "How does it serve me to use this form of power with others?" You might at first say, "It doesn't serve me." Go deeper with your inquiry. What do you get from using power in this way? What are you avoiding? Of what are you afraid people will decide or find out about you if you were to show up without this form of power? What would they see?
- List any event, circumstance or environment in which you have this particular belief: clients, children, husband, phone company, computer, weather, etc.
- Are you willing to consider other ways of relating to the people with whom you come into contact?

  To notice how one is being in relation to personal use of power cultivates awareness and perhaps an awakening. Be open to the practice of opening to possibility and what may come of that.

Chapter 2: Success

We are entering another domain—with the conversation about power behind us—that causes so many people to choose less than satisfying lives. The intention of this chapter is for you to decide honestly how you want to *be* in relation to success in every aspect of your life. By clarifying what you say you want and by distinguishing how you are willing to be with success, you can then choose to be fiercely intentional in the way that supports you. You can choose also to be more compassionate with yourself as you determine what you want and how you will be with the consequences of acquiring or achieving it. You will see how you may be creating interference with your work in order to avoid success or too much success.

What is Success

The most basic of definitions of success is the achievement of stated goals or desired outcomes. When you have realized your intention, success is the outcome. With that said; however, your interpretation of success is far more compelling and is that which directs and motivates your actions.

COACHING QUESTIONS: *What shows up with the idea of success? What beliefs and interpretations do you have about success? What shows up as a felt-sense in your body when you think of success? What would shift if you were allowed to decide what success looked like for yourself and you lived into that decision?*

We have an idea of what success is supposed to look like. We are clobbered with it every day. Flawless physical beauty, enormous wealth, a passionate career, the perfect relationship, higher education, ideal children, deep spirituality, every aspect of our lives is ruled by some determinant that tells us if we are successful or not. Looking at your home, children, job; from a cultural perspective that includes your parents, friends and associates; do you see reflections of your interpretation of success or have you met someone else's expectations of success? Either way, it challenges your self-esteem, self-worth, self-value and your personal truth and power. My little 26-foot travel trailer has been my home for four years. It doesn't meet the requirements of success in my book, or anyone else's, I imagine; however, it allows me a wonderful lifestyle that includes living on an exquisite and beautiful island in the Pacific Northwest and a home in California. So, it isn't my home that reflects my success, but my ability to enjoy my chosen lifestyle.

Though most of us say we are out to be successful, many of us limit and sabotage our personal and professional success unwittingly. To what are we responding that would have us say we want to be successful and then come up short consistently? It is ironic that we work so hard to look *as if* we are being successful and at the same time, we are putting the kibosh on it. This occurs not only in relation to our work and career, but also in relation to our health, partners—everything. Rarely, it is related to competence or resources, but most often to our interpretations about ourselves and to that which we say we want.

Success is a relative term in reference to where you are and where you are going. As you participate actively in your life and career, you can't help, but bump up against the edges of your own comfort zone. You will bump into frustration and anxiety because your life or career isn't going where you expected or anticipated. You will bump up against excitement too because you are expanding yourself actively to fulfill that which you say you want. Either way, being with success and power is an uninterrupted practice of being with anxiety. You will fight and resist or you will allow its presence and relate to it not as something that threatens you, but something that encourages your fullest attention and commitment.

This drive for power and success is a crucial facet of being human; however, it is crucial as well that you choose how you want to *be* with this drive consciously, either through healthy interplay or intimidation and fear-based exchanges. Your capacity to be with anxiety will determine your ability to create successfully the outcomes that you desire.

As a coach, viewing my clients from outside their context—their story of the truth—it is easy to see how they limit their success. By addressing with them the diverse ways they do this, each client begins to access different practices that shift what, at the outset seemed impossible, to being possible. They decide what success looks like for them and begin to take action that moves them closer to fulfilling that picture. They move into unknown territory that can elicit various levels of fear and anxiety. This gives them the opportunity to exercise courage in order to be with uncomfortable body sensations, emotions and thoughts that they normally avoid through distractions, diversions. Through the practice of being with this exploration, they begin to find that things change and they are able to be with the experience of success in a new way.

To What Degree Are You Committed to Being Successful

Without thinking about it and just off the top of your head, how would you rate yourself on a scale of zero to 100 about your level of commitment to your success in general? If you are 100% committed in earnest, I propose you will have the success you want and are doing everything it takes to make that success yours. Most of us would be lying if we said we were committed 100%.

There are varying degrees of commitment. Most of us are somewhere on the scale between one and 100%. I am at about 87% committed to success. What about the other 13%, you might ask. The other 13% is committed to being lazy and doing nothing, but having fun. This aspect had me procrastinating on finishing this book or writing articles and many other things that might bring more clients and more speaking engagements. This part of me wants to stay home and take naps in my hammock. It resists taking time away from *enjoying* life. It worries that if I get too successful, I won't have much time to do just nothing. It's being afraid of the responsibilities that may come with the success of my career. Will I still be successful in my work? Yes! Will I have obstacles stop me or slow me down? Absolutely. These obstacles show up because I have interpretations about success that limits my commitment that then limits what I do and when I do it.

One of my trainees, Celeste, shared with me, "I want a career that is successful in providing me with a great income and great clients and at the same time, I want flexibility, freedom and fun." Celeste is learning through her practice that if this is truly, what she wants, this is what she can create. Are there consequences? Yes. Are the consequences bad or scary? No! Like Celeste, you have what it takes to create the life and career just as you want it, but you have to decide how committed you are to your career, spouse, health and finances being successful and how committed you are to being successful at *not* being successful. You cannot *not* be successful at being successful or you can be successful at not being successful. These are the only two choices you have.

Growing your success means a couple of things: first, recognizing and acknowledging your present level of commitment to success and second, recognizing and acknowledging that you have a commitment to some belief or idea that may directly oppose your commitment to success. This conflicting commitment is related often to staying safe, avoiding the feeling of anxiety, avoiding vulnerability and avoiding responsibility.

Are You Growing It, Killing It or Letting It Die

If you think seriously about what you want in relation to success, you will want to ask yourself this question; are you growing your success, killing it or letting it die? This very powerful question distinguishes how you are *being* in relation to your success. It allows you to be at choice on whether you want to grow the relationship, kill it or let it die. No one in their right mind would be out to kill their success while at the same time *trying* to build a career or relationship; however, you would be surprised at the degree to which almost every one of us is doing that exactly.

How you are *being* in relation to success will either support success or limit its development or (*read this carefully)* **you will create something that looks like failure**, but you would not have actually failed. It is just that you were honoring a commitment to something other than success and you killed your own potential unconsciously and intentionally. Getting clear about whether you are growing, killing or letting your success die is crucial in the conversation regarding your level of commitment to being successful. You can be as successful at ruining your career, diet or finances as you can be at actualizing one that has fulfillment and meaning.

Killing His Practice

Stan, a coaching trainee, has completed almost all of the requirements for his certification of completion from his training program. He moved mountains, over the course of his training, to grow into who he is in relation to himself, his partners and friends. I witnessed Stan shift how he was *being* to allow more vulnerability and a more authentic expression of himself. It was a pleasure to see him blossom into a more joyful human being. He brought more of himself to each coaching session as he blossomed and allowed room for his clients to bring more of their authentic self and their truth to each session. Stan's career as a coach looked like it would soar, but something happened. Stan declared that he was committed to attracting more *paying* clients. With that, a big, fat void showed up in his business as a coach. The people with whom he had been working completed their work and no one else was there to fill his calendar. His well of clients dried up quickly and he was left high and dry. Stan became frustrated and anxious from this turn of events and worried that no one would be willing to pay him for his services. He returned to being angry, resistant and used his old blaming strategies for dealing with his lack of success. So, to stave off his anxiety about being an unsuccessful coach, he decided to become a physical trainer with a lucrative health club from which he would have more security.

Those of us who have created a successful private practice know there is a time when seeing clients on a sliding scale and sometimes for free is a good thing to do. It gives coaches a chance to practice with a client developing confidence and competence. It lets clients experience the value of coaching. From there the clients can share that experience with their friends. Free work can create new referrals. Even in the most lucrative practices, most practitioners provide some degree of pro-bono work because they enjoy giving to those in need.

Stan put his foot down and as a result, shot it. He made the decision to stop seeing clients on a pro-bono basis much too early in his career. Was he growing his practice and success, killing his practice or letting his practice die?

It appears that his intention was to grow his practice by seeing only clients who paid, but from the viewpoint of those who witnessed this process, we saw him killing a huge potential for success.

Had Stan developed a good foundation of clients before making his decision, things might have looked different; however, he was just beginning to experience success with himself and his clients. He had a couple of other jobs that helped support him while he developed his practice, yet he made the choice he made to his own detriment.

Stan stopped getting coached and stopped getting support for his practice as a coach. He stopped allowing the flow of success to come to him. I think he got scared of what would show up if he really became successful and so, returned to his old survival strategies killing his potential as a coach. Stan had a particular interpretation of what success looked like and his actions were based on that.

An addendum to this story is; over the past two years, Stan has found more satisfaction and fulfillment in his work than he anticipated. He expanded his comfort zone to include a deeper appreciation for his intellect and joy of learning. He is intentional about what is of value in terms of his life's work and continues to follow his passion. He doesn't know where it will lead him, but he is having more fun in the adventure of finding out.

What Does Success Mean to You

People often resist that which makes them feel uncomfortable.

COACHING QUESTIONS: *What belief or interpretation do you have about success? Which of these beliefs creates an emotional or physical response in you that stops you from moving forward toward success? How do you* be *with these feelings? What do you do to avoid these feelings?*

Melissa, a first time novelist wanted to be more successful at selling her book. When asked about her belief about success, she had this to say, "Success means the horse will run away with me and the cart. I don't trust that I can handle everything that comes with the success of my book."

Like Melissa, so many of us resist success because it means our practice, business and lives will be unmanageable and uncontrollable. There won't be enough time with partners, family or friends. There are a large number of individuals who think there is too much responsibility with success.

Carolyn, one of my clients, believes that success takes a lot of hard work. She doesn't want to feel deprived by working so much and limiting time for fun. She says, "When I think about success, I get afraid that I will have less time for solitude, less time at home and more time being exhausted and overwhelmed. It doesn't seem possible that I could take on more when what I'm doing already seems like too much."

Do you think Melissa and Carolyn, with their particular perceptions and interpretations about success, will grow their success, kill their success or let their success die?

For some reason, it felt impossible to have the level of success they said they wanted and still have all the time they wanted for other and important aspects of their lives. Given their present circumstances, financially and otherwise, it feels impossible. Guess what? They created a scenario that matched their expectations. When things feel impossible, most of us set our sights lower to what seems more manageable, less vulnerable and risky, and possible.

COACHING QUESTIONS: *Based on what success means to you, what do you do? Do you worry? Do you get anxious? Do you resist moving forward through procrastination, illness or accidents? Do you avoid, deny or detract yourself from that which you say you are going to do, or do you get excited and create a plan of action that you implement? Do you do something every day that moves you closer to success, just because you say so, even though it feels scary and uncomfortable?*

Getting clearer about what is true for you about success and what you do based on what is true will give you a picture of what is supporting success for you and what is limiting it. What we think and feel is based on our interpretations and our actions follow directly behind. These two elements put together create both what is possible and what is impossible in relation to success.

Killing Success

We sabotage our possibility of success in so many different ways. I can come up with a hundred different was to avoid finishing this book and each of them are legitimate. I can kill this project in a heartbeat. I can let it die in the midst of doing all the other things that need my attention or I can continue to grow this book one day at a time, one fear-facing moment at a time, one action at a time, one word at a time, and one success at a time.

I look around and see many people who are desperate for work and money. I see people who are writing books and are unsuccessful at getting them published. These observations can discourage me or I can say to myself, "Well, there are thousands of people out there actually being very successful at writing and publishing. If they can do it, why can't I?"

The bottom line is; if others are doing it, it is not impossible! The question is; what is it that has some people create success and others create what looks like failure?

Fearing the Consequences of Success

We want what we want. At the same time, we don't want the consequences that we imagine come along with what we say we want. Like you, my students and clients had to decide what they really wanted. I hear, "I want success, but I don't want the consequences that come along with it. I don't want to spend a lot of time being responsible for the business and financial part of the business. I don't want to deal with the money part of my practice. I don't want to deal with renting an office or sharing space with someone else. I'll have to get a telephone, web site, cards and brochures. I'll have to meet people and sell/market myself." It all sounds overwhelming inside your head. It sounds as though it is too much to handle.

People focus too often on the negative consequences of their success. They spend more energy worrying and being afraid than they do on feeling the exhilaration of actually doing what they say they love to do. The focus is on what seems impossible and so it becomes a self-fulfilling prophecy. They either kill their dreams or let them die a slow and agonizing death.

Just Being with What Is

You may be feeling a little anxious as we distinguish aspects of this phase of creating success. There are details to consider and take care of and there is plenty of support for you, support that is affordable and available whatever your endeavor.

When I began to develop my practice, I started with what was doable at the time. I had a financial budget and this budget was created in relation to my *comfort zone* and my time. Developing a practice and a career is stepping into the unknown, something that is not yet tangible. I was becoming someone different as I related to the world based on who I was becoming. I was treading out beyond what was known, exploring and investigating what I wanted and who I was in relation to what I wanted. I could see, along the way that I wanted to collapse and say, "I can't do this." I didn't have enough energy for creating my cards and brochures. Little by little, I enjoyed finding out that I was capable of so much more than I thought possible. All of the consequences of beginning a practice were just things to *be* with so I could also be with the things I loved and enjoyed. Do you want success enough to *be* with some of the consequences that will show up? What will you choose to choose?

I was seeing clients for over a year before I got my business cards made and these cards I made myself on my computer. Another two years elapsed before I was willing to hire someone to help me create a logo and a card that truly represented my business and me. My brochure is always being recreated as I move into different stages of personal and professional development. My web site too is always growing and changing. Your practice will constantly evolve as you do. As you grow, so will your relationships to people, money and work.

I hated thinking about money. I never really knew what was in my checking account. I would play a guessing game with it and most of the time I would win, but this particular strategy wasn't enhancing my practice, nor was it enhancing my accountability. I read somewhere that it is a good practice to let other people do what they love to do and to let yourself do what you love to do. That's when I realized that I could pay people to take care of things I didn't want to do. Even though it meant an outflow of money, it also meant I had more time to make money the way I like. It meant I had more free time to relax and have fun. Now, my bookkeeper takes care of my receipts and records, my accountant does my taxes, I have an editor for my writing and I have hired a personal assistant to take care of details that take time away from of my writing, seeing my clients and facilitating trainings, workshops and retreats.

My attitude about money has changed too. In the beginning, I believed that the consequences of being successful meant that I would have to fork out money to hire people to help me. I used to think, "What is the point of making money if it is just going to fly out the window?" Now, I really enjoy supporting people financially as they support me in creating my wants and desires. This was a gigantic shift in my interpretation of success. I'm having a lot of fun creating possibilities for hiring people to do what they love while I do what I love. Instead of the consequences looking dismal and scary, I find that they continue to provide a win-win situation for everyone. It is just a matter of stepping into the practice of working with what appears to be impossible.

Where I was in the beginning of my practice is not where I am now. I grew myself into the level of success to which I was committed. I paid attention to when and where I would get distracted and avoid responsibility. I had to decide where to focus my energy and actions. I became vigilant in making sure that my anxiety and fears didn't divert me off my path. I listened for all of the little voices in my head that said I wasn't good enough and didn't deserve the success I wanted. These were the saboteurs of my success. If others can do it, I can do it! If I can do it, *you can* do it! It comes down to two words: accountability and integrity.

Accountability and Integrity

Within the statement, "I will start tomorrow," is an inherent statement of ***accountability and integrity.*** To me, these two words mean that you mean what you say and you say what you mean. You do what you do because you say so; no other reason is necessary. You can count on yourself for following through. You, being able to count on yourself is *the* most important thing. Others will be able to count on you to follow through on your word.

I am working with a number of clients who are just starting their business. Together, we create a plan of action and then the clients leave with full intentions of taking care of the details. It is not unusual for them to return with little or no fulfillment of their practice areas. They didn't follow through. They didn't do what they said they would do. What is missing?

We have many rationalizations, justifications and excuses for not following through and not being successful, but rationalization and justifications are not the same as having been accountable to others and yourself. One of the values of having a coach is that you have someone to whom you are accountable, someone with whom to talk through the resistance and immobility. Like Stan who decided on his own to stop working with the people who weren't paying, most of us keep our own counsel and; therefore, limit opportunities for following through with the integrity and accountability. Without accountability and integrity, you will probably be extremely successful at creating failure.

When a client comes in without having made any progress, I know they are in alignment with some underlying or conflicting commitment; maybe to staying small, avoiding success or hiding out. Through conversations, we bring saboteurs into the light and disempower them. My client is then free to choose the pursuit of success over the pursuit of success in failing, staying small and hiding out.

Being Successful at Marketing and Selling Yourself

Marketing and selling yourself as an entrepreneur, executive, employee of any sort or as someone looking for a significant life partner, is the best practice to take in order to observe how you are being in integrity and being accountable about growing yourself in relation to what you say you want. You'll notice yourself trying to kill your dream or just let it die. It challenges the best of us to look at our motivating beliefs of who we are and the work we are bringing into the world. You have to be who you say you are; otherwise, at some point people will see you as a fraud and decide that you aren't who they thought you were and they will be right. They will see how you hide out and *be* something other than who you say you are.

People stop themselves from putting themselves out there because of the potential exposure of being found out. Marketing and selling takes place whether you want a career, an intimate relationship or a social life; you have to put yourself out there!

COACHING QUESTIONS: *What are you afraid people will find out about you? Will they find out that you are hiding your incompetence, insecurities and fears or will they*

find out that you are hiding your brilliance, creativity and ability to make a difference in the world? What is it that has you be less than 100% accountable to yourself and your life?

There are internal dialogs that stop each of us and get in the way of actualizing our careers, relationships and to, well… just about everything. You can look at CEO's around the world and each will have some degree of fear and anxiety about how much success they can handle. We've seen many executives who try too hard at being successful and tumble to the ground, not because they were failures, but because they weren't willing to be accountable in their position of power. Their demise had nothing to do with incompetence, but with an unwillingness to face themselves with a different context of success. We have the capacity to succeed and we have the capacity to fail miserably. It's just a matter of choice.

I teach a course at the Institute of Transpersonal Psychology called *Transformational Coaching*. The question asked most often is, "How do I market myself successfully?" Nine of 10 times though, the challenging conversation is not about *how to*, but most often about the dialog inside the coach's head that stops them from putting themselves out there. It is about how they are *being* with the thought of marketing and selling themselves and their services. How they are *being* with letting other people know they offer something valuable, themselves and their work. The dialog going on inside their heads is the obstacle interfering with doing whatever it takes to be successful in bringing clients to their door.

In the business world, it may look as though the external world is not cooperating with your desire for success. It may look as though people are not responding to your brilliant brochures, web sites and business cards. It may also look as though they are not responding to your articles or to your networking. In your personal world, it may seem as though there isn't a soul interested in you, even after all the effort you put into developing yourself, in order to appear to be that perfect partner. It may appear as though people just don't want what you have to offer. By distinguishing the underlying conversations going on inside your head, you can begin to reveal concerns about risking your identity and risking the security of your comfort zone. It becomes obvious how you may be sabotaging success through this process.

I hear clients say too often that they are afraid people will find out or decide that they are a fake or a fraud. They worry about the responsibility of being with potential partners, friends or clients. Each of them worries about losing the freedom and flexibility they've enjoyed. Each of these individuals turn their thoughts into actions that will have them suffer, settle or survive their current circumstances and limit their potential for further success.

Human beings are fascinating. We want a career badly enough to spend thousands of dollars for education and training, then we get in our own way by not allowing the manifestation of our desires. We want to be attractive to potential partners enough to spend enormous amounts of time, money and energy to beautify ourselves then sabotage any possibility of relationship by listening to that voice in our head that says we'll never have what it takes to have the love of our lives. When we reveal the underlying conversations that undermine our momentum and success, we can begin to be different with these internal dialogs. We can shift our thoughts, attitudes and actions that follow, and in no time, we find to our own surprise, there are plenty of individuals who want what we have to offer; our authentic, essential self and all the gifts and talents we've developed out of love and passion for life.

A Case In Point: Veronica

For the last two years, Veronica, a client of mine has been traveling between Washington to Italy, taking a training program in a specialized form of meditation. She will finish her certificate soon. Veronica broke down crying at our last session. "I'm sad and I'm scared," she said through intermittent sobs. "I am so close to finishing my training and I am afraid I won't be good at leading groups. I'm afraid no one will come and I am afraid I won't make any money at this."

Veronica is in her late fifties. Over her lifetime, she has been a health practitioner and social worker. By attending many workshops, Veronica has been striving to bring more tools and skills to her work, but she wants this particular training to be the last. She wants to be enough now without further pursuit of skill building; however, at this moment, she doesn't feel yet that she is enough or has enough skills to attract and keep clients in her groups.

Revealing the Expert She Is

We distinguished through our sessions that her fear of not being good enough as a group facilitator is independent of her fear of having people show up to her groups and is also independent of her fear that her work won't support her financially. It hadn't occurred to her before this session that these were all different aspects of what she considered success.

We began by exploring and identifying all the different ways Veronica had created her expertise in the work she wanted to do. She listed all the various skills she developed and all the experience she had accrued. It became clear that because of her years of training and experience with people, she was well prepared to lead groups. Veronica sighed and began to relax. The evidence of her success as a practitioner outweighed her illusion that she didn't have enough experience to offer her clients. From here, we moved on to the next issue.

Attracting Clients

We tackled the underlying conversation supporting Veronica's fear about clients actually attending her groups. This was a bit more challenging to ground. As with all of us, Veronica's external world was seductive and provocative. It seemed as if it was telling her how she would do in relation to success as a practitioner. In some ways, it does and in some ways, it reflects only the limiting beliefs Veronica has about herself, her work and her environment.

Much like any of us facing a new career, Veronica has fears that undermine her success. Her low sense of self-worth and value comes across strongly in any marketing endeavor she employs. Mistakes in her advertisements, notices of events running late and procrastination when delivering her offerings are some ways she keeps from putting herself out there with confidence and clarity of intention. Veronica realized that when she follows her fears, there isn't much attraction to the beautiful work she has to offer. One item on Veronica's list for success is having people come to her groups. If she isn't grounded in her values and the values of her work, she will continue to sabotage her success and people will not show up at her door.

It is challenging to talk about the vibrational nature of our reality without sounding *woo-woo*, but like Veronica, we put ourselves out there in a way that reflects not who we are, but who we *think* we are. Then we attract people to us or deter people from coming anywhere near us. Not every individual is meant to be your client or your partner. You will have a particular style and special field of practice that will attract the people with whom you are meant to work. Your clients will find you *if* you are open to receiving them.

When I began the pursuit of a *private practice*, I learned that it takes anywhere from two to five years to develop a full and successful practice. Though my practice was healthy and thriving after three years, I didn't give up worrying about having enough clients until I'd been working for nearly five years. I was still operating under limiting beliefs about myself and about my work. Limiting beliefs create limitations. I perceived myself as struggling and not having enough; therefore, I experienced struggle and not having enough. I was able—with the support of a financial coach—to recognize how my perceptions of being financially unsuccessful created my experience of struggle and lack. To shift this perceived circumstance, I had to practice experiencing the success I had achieved and allow myself to embrace the evidence that showed I did create a thriving practice. I had to be willing to see myself as successful instead of someone trying to be successful. This huge distinction allowed me to relax into my success.

Gathering Evidence

I believe that it is one thing to do the right things to get known and get referrals. It's another thing to actually grow and develop yourself personally and professionally to the degree that you are willing to attract more and more clients; that you are willing to own the success you have created; that you are willing to acknowledge your ability to create that which you say you want.

Sure, there are those individuals who have what it takes to create a full practice instantaneously; however, more often than not, most of us must reinterpret ourselves in relation to self-worth and the value of the work we are bringing to the world. Instead of gathering evidence that supports incompetence and unworthiness, we have to be willing to gather evidence that we are enough and that what we do is enough—more than enough.

So many people are working unhappily for agencies and organizations because they don't want to face the fears that keep them from actualizing their dreams. The same fears that keep us settling for a job that is less than satisfying, could be the same fears that keep us settling for relationships with friends, family, partners, children, health and wealth that are also less than satisfying. These fears do not go away until they are revealed and exposed for what they are—just thoughts and feelings we made up somewhere along our life path. We created these thoughts and feelings so we can un-create them.

I encourage you to face your fears head-on. You will realize the amazing gifts that are waiting to be shared with the world!

Back to Veronica

Veronica's brain worked hard to grasp new ways of perceiving her old beliefs around how her low *self-worth* interfered with participants coming to her groups. She understood that the level of success regarding people coming to her groups and staying was related to her commitment to herself and her work. She needed to own the true value of the work she had been preparing to do her whole life. She needed to live into the momentum that carried her to this moment in her career. She needed to maintain the level of inspiration that carried her to Italy for the training. She needed to focus on the evidence that she *had what it took* to create a successful practice.

Fear About Making Enough Money

Veronica's list of fears had one last issue to tackle. It was her fear of not making enough money doing what she loved. Like her relationship to potential clients, Veronica's relationship to money is completely unrelated to her success as a leader of groups. Her relationship with money is a separate issue altogether.

When I asked Veronica how much money she would like to make from her career as a group facilitator, she thought hard for a moment and then said very shyly, “Umm, $20,000?” Twenty-thousand dollars is not much money on which to live anywhere in the United States. “Think about making $30,000.” I pressed. “How does that feel?” Veronica became a bit more animated and said, “That would be nice. I would be able to go on vacations and do more fun things.” I pressed one more time, “What about $35,000?” I said. Veronica shrank into her chair, as if from the sheer weight alone of so much money. “That feels like too much responsibility to be making that amount of money. I don’t know that I want that kind of responsibility.”

Veronica has created a lifestyle based partly on her avoidance of responsibility. Though she has been successful as a social worker and body worker, she has at the same time, lived in relative poverty, intentionally. She has done so because her interpretations about money are too stressful to consider.

We will be talking about this more in the following chapters, but for now, it’s important to see that Veronica’s conditions of success have little to do with her external circumstances and more to do with her motivation to shift her sense of value as a person, as a facilitator and her willingness to shift her relationship with money.

Six months after this session, Veronica continues to exhibit the shifts that need to occur for her groups to be successful. Her physical presence reflects more confidence and self-value. She speaks with more clarity and purpose. She is having more fun in her life, looking more relaxed and refreshed. She is attracting people to her groups and individual sessions and is enjoying the success she set out to create.

The ability to have a positive relationship with success, as with power, is based solely on your interpretations, your own meaning of the word. To grow your relationship with success you must first reveal your interpretations of success, recognizing them for what they are and how they serve you. Second, be willing to practice something different just to see if you get the results, you would like while handling the *negative* consequences effortlessly. Finally, acknowledge the evidence indicating that you have created the level of success you wanted. Part of the practice is noticing and acknowledging the evidence that you may be killing success, letting it die or creating the illusions of failure for you and the world to see.

Creating Yourself as a Failure

By now, you can see that I believe strongly, we make use of our power to create ourselves as failures as easily as we use it to create ourselves as successes. Do you gather evidence to prove the case that you are a success or a failure? Most of us do both to one degree or another. Yet, when seeking evidence for failure, people have a very challenging time naming specific failures. When they do, it is quite easy to see that what they have done is sabotage their success by failing intentionally to stay safe and avoid vulnerability.

Through revealing the conversation about success and failure, every one of my clients recognized how invested they had been in limiting their success. They saw that their practice of failing was just a way of avoiding their fantasies of what might evolve with their success. We all use our creative power to create failure as effectively as creating success. It's up to each one of us to decide how we want to use our power.

Fierce Compassion

How do we *be* fierce and compassionate with ourselves in the face of creating the level of success we want? Throughout a lifetime, each one of us will have a unique human experience that unfolds moment by moment. We are secure in our assumptions that we have a handle on how it's all going to turn out. At the same time, if the truth be known, we don't know. We are stepping off a precipice every morning we awake and put our feet on the floor. We take leaps of faith every waking moment.

Creating yourself as who you want to be can be anxiety provoking; you have no idea what your fullest potential looks like. Are you curious enough to take the adventure? Are you courageous enough to endure anxious moments of not knowing for the sake of finding out? Can you be fierce enough with yourself that you practice the discipline of accountability, living into integrity and aligning your actions with your highest truth? Can you be compassionate with yourself through this exploration, allowing yourself to fumble and be humbled by this amazing process of finding your *highest self, highest truth* and *highest potential?* Can you be compassionate enough with yourself to reach out for handholds, supports and resources that allow your strengths to be seen and acknowledged? You are not alone! There are so many resources out there waiting for you to want your life enough, enough to reach beyond your perceived limitations. Holding yourself accountable while holding yourself with compassion is your practice. Being real with your life and your circumstances is what is required for full success to reveal itself to you one moment at a time.

Practice Areas

- List 25 things you have accomplished that indicate you have the capacity to create success in your life.
- Which areas of your life have you created most successfully? What allowed you to create success in these specific areas? What inner processes did you resource to create this success? Can you access that resource now to support you in being successful in a different arena of your life?
- What, if anything, was threatening to you in creating success in the past? What is in the way of creating success in this present endeavor? In what ways can you empower yourself to be successful?
- Create a description or picture of what success looks like and feels like to you. Be as specific as possible. You might create a collage or use paints or clay to give your image some dimension.
- With this description in mind, what are you afraid people will decide or find out about you if you actualize this into reality? In what ways do you sabotage your success so people won't find out or decide this about you?
- Are you committed enough to your success that you will hire a coach or join a support group today? If the answer is no, to what are you committed that stops you? If it's about money, read on…

Chapter 3: Money

How Do You Be with Money

COACHING QUESTIONS: *How do you be with money? Are you being connected, invested and enthusiastic in your relationship with money or are you being distracted, unfocused, troubled, anxious and guilty in your relationship with money? Where else in your life are you connected, invested and enthusiastic? Where else in your life do you avoid, distract and deny? In which areas are you finding more success and fulfillment? Of those areas, which are connected, invested and enthusiastic or where you are distracted, troubled, stressed, anxious and worried?*

By answering these questions, you will reveal a pattern of being with money that may change your life significantly.

Cameron

Cameron is a brilliant individual with a huge amount of training and expertise in her field as a psychologist. She has been in practice for about 25 years and has raised her fees once only in that time. She requested coaching around feeling tired and burnt out. She wanted to see if there was another way to be in practice where she didn't have to work so many hours.

Of course, the subject of increasing her fees came up early in our conversation, as a possibility to reduce client hours and still maintain her present income. I could tell by the look on her face that she had a ready-made image in her head holding her hostage when thinking of a rate increase. Cameron revealed particular beliefs, through our exploration that she'd held onto for decades. Her context around money had been limiting any possibility to charge what she was worth and allow freedom and flexibility with her time.

She has two basic truths regarding a fee raise. Truth #1 – "Any psychologist, therapist and those serving the public should not charge more than what people can afford. If they do then they are money-hungry and money-gouging." I could see the angst in her whole body as she talked about this. The word *gouging* made her cringe in her chair. It's as if she wanted to disappear into the upholstery. Truth #2 – "It isn't saintly to be asking for more money than you need."

Now, looking at Cameron's living situation, you would wonder about a number of things. She has been divorced for six years and her children are grown and have families of their own. She has been living in a small apartment, one barely big enough for her small office, for the past six years. She has a Ph.D. spent thousands of dollars on her education and training. She lives like a pauper. It's not hard to see that Cameron's living situation is a reflection of her truths.

Being outside Cameron's story, one can see clearly that Cameron is operating from a belief system that limits her ability to change her fee structure. By doing so, she believes she would be an un-saintly, money-hungry gouger. Raised in a Catholic family where charity was espoused, she decided that it was better to minimize her needs rather than deal with the question of her own value and self-worth. Other people's value came before hers. This is how it was in her childhood, this is how it was as a mother and wife and this is how it is with her clients. Cameron has been diminishing her own well-being for the sake of avoiding the internal conflict around taking care of her own needs first in order to be more available and present to those she serves. This reminds me of the spiel flight attendants give about oxygen masks. They make it very clear that parents need to put their masks on first so they will have the capacity to support their children putting on theirs. If we, as caregivers are not taking care of ourselves first, eventually we lose our capacity to take care of others.

The degree to which Cameron is committed to her limiting beliefs is the degree to which she will be unable to shift and take the necessary actions that would follow. She has history and practice living within these truths. Is she willing to practice something different, perhaps based on some other truths that are part of her context around fees and money?

"What might be another truth you believe about your clients?" I asked Cameron. She responded slowly, clarifying her thoughts as she spoke. "Well, first and foremost, I'm a professional and my practice has been pretty successful, I think, because of my professionalism."

"Sitting in your professionalism chair and not in the saintly one; tell me about fees and money." I asked.

Her posture shifted immediately. Her back straightened, her neck elongated, her eyes became focused and clear. Her whole demeanor shifted. "As a professional, I'm clear, intentional, grounded and in integrity. My fees reflect my ability to serve my clients. When I am serving my clients from a place of vitality, health and well-being, my clients get so much more value than when I'm tired, worn out, hungry and stressed. I serve my clients best when I serve myself first." She finished her last statement and then looked at me with shock at what came out of her mouth. "Wow! That's a whole other side of me that I haven't heard before. That feels good to say that. From this place I see how I can and even need to raise my fees in order to really live into being the professional that I am."

Here is a place where so many of us get confused. Cameron's conversation reflects two aspects of her that counter each other. She has the side of her that is entrenched in a belief that says she can't raise her fees or she will be guilty of being a money-hungry gouger. The other side of her says she is a professional whose effectiveness is a result of her creating well-being that most likely includes raising her fees. How does she *be* with this dilemma? How will she *be* with these conflicting sets of truths?

The Money Conversation

People's relationship with money is one of the most fascinating phenomena's and influences in the realm of their power and achievement. Our beliefs, interpretations assumptions and expectations about money are amazing and significant. By living in these beliefs, we generate so much of what shows up in our lives. We emphasize their importance and give them tremendous power to make us feel successful or make us feel like failures. We give them the power to make us happy, anxious, worried, depressed or diseased. In some cases, we give them the power to kill us.

The intention of this chapter is to identify the significance and meaning you have assigned to money that either enhances your desire to cultivate a successful life or slow you down, perhaps stopping you altogether.

We have developed specific beliefs and patterns of behaving in relation to money. Most of us would like to have more money, but for some reason it just doesn't seem to be flowing into our pockets. At the same time, we may see other people making money effortlessly. We make up stories about all of this, thinking that perhaps we are victims of circumstances and fate. We continue wishing and hoping and at the same time, we may feel powerless to have it any different.

If The Truth Be Known

There is so much scientific evidence today pointing to the truth; we are *not* victims of circumstance or fate. We are victims of our perceptions, interpretations and beliefs. This is becoming mainstream knowledge. Even Oprah Winfrey devoted an entire program to the Law of Attraction. She had a panel of experts speaking about how we create our reality through acting on our beliefs and perceptions.

All of this scientific evidence is based on quantum physics and the nature of a tiny and invisible particle that is attracted to a vibrational field that brings it into form. We create a vibrational field, in relation to anything we think about and right now, as we are talking about money, we are creating a particular vibrational field, based on what we are thinking and feeling about money. How you perceive money, what you think about prosperity, poverty, scarcity and abundance and how you *be* emotionally with it will be what shows up in your pocket, bank account and your investment portfolio.

What Money Is Really

Let's look at the truth about money. Money is just paper and metal—***paper and metal!*** Think about that for a moment. Take a sheet of paper from your printer and look at it. It is just paper. Now, look at the metal of a tin can. It is just metal, but someone a long time ago decided that instead of carrying around furs and sacks of flour for trade, we would use paper and metal to represent a trade of furs for flour. Our bartering metal was weighted by the gold standard. Now paper and metal's value is only what we give it. It represents an exchange of value for value only. That's it!

Somehow, this particular meaning was assigned to paper and metal and over time, more significance and power was added. When we give something significance, we give it power. When we give something power, we are also deciding whether it gives *us* power or *diminishes* our power.

Back to Power and the Significance We Assign It

I was walking down a little road last week and spotted the remains of a dead rabbit. Bits of fur, blood and a rabbit's foot were off to the side of the path, waiting for the next scavenger to have its meal. When I saw the rabbit's foot, my thoughts jumped immediately to the significance many people give the foot as a lucky charm. "What's so lucky about a rabbit's foot?" I asked myself. "Who gave this little creature's appendage such importance? It's just a dead animal's foot. How did it get translated into something lucky?" I can create a story to suggest how a hungry hunter caught a rabbit, felt lucky and decided to carry the rabbit's foot with him as a charm to bring more rabbits his way. Whatever the truth may be, the outcome is that people carry around rabbit's feet as lucky charms.

The power and significance put on this little furry foot often changes people's lives. If they *believe* it is lucky, then they see good things happen. By giving something significance, we give it meaning and power and set up this vibrational field, I had mentioned earlier, then good things happen. So too, with money.

It's Not About the Money

"IT'S NOT ABOUT THE MONEY! IT'S NEVER ABOUT MONEY!" I hear my friend Kelly hollering at me.

It took me many years to get what Kelly was telling me. It's not about the money; it's about your interpretations about money and it's about your relationship to yourself in relationship to money. Making it about the money is like making it about the rabbit's foot.

The Context Around Everything

Let's get down to business! Everything has an environment or context within which it occurs. A context is a container; parameters of truth within which we think, sense, feel and take action. Our thinking, feeling and action are based on what we consider true, which includes our beliefs, assumptions and expectations—every interpretation we have about every topic we've ever considered or thought. These perceptions, interpretations and our actions set up a vibrational field that supports particular outcomes to be possible and other outcomes to be impossible. Within our given context, we are swimming in a fishbowl of beliefs. Our fishbowl is our reality and we may have no sense that there is an ocean of possibility available to us beyond the parameters of our beliefs.

What Does It Take

What does it take to shift any powerful paradigm that holds you hostage around power, success or money? It takes just three things:

1. Look at the evidence from an objective perspective. That means stepping out of your fishbowl so you can see it from the outside, take off the filters on your proverbial lenses and be willing to see things differently.
2. Look at the beliefs and interpretations that create your specific reality about money and the manifestation that follows.
3. Decide to choose differently if what you want is different than what you have.

Are there people who are happy and successful who are making money? Yes! If they can do it, so can you! I can hear you add, "Yes, but…" STOP! Stop the, "Ycs, but's…" NOW! You have been doing that all of your life. How is it working for you to "yes, but" everything? You can always point to other people's circumstances being different than yours and think that's why they are where they are and you are where you are. It goes both ways. You can point to your dysfunctional family, abusive math teacher, your lisp or the mole on your left hip. You can always find reasons, rationalizations and justifications to have not, be not, do not—toward what it is you say you want, but for some reason are avoiding. There are people who have it better than you and there are people who have it worse. You can point to the evidence that says you can't and you can point to the evidence that says you can. CHOOSE! To which will you point? Which one will take you the direction in which you want to go? Evidence says you can make the money you want and still have love, happiness, joy, freedom and fun. Is that what you really want and are you willing to do what it takes to have it? (This is the point, my friend Kelly was trying to teach me. It's not about the money. It's your interpretation about the money.)

The following exercise allows you to see the fishbowl in which you are swimming, in relation to money. It's an opportunity to see how you perceive and interpret yourself, other people and your world within the context of money.

This exercise allows you to reveal the connection between your own personal beliefs and the outcomes that follow. These outcomes may be particular thoughts, feelings and body sensations as well as actions, behaviors and circumstances that continually show up in your life. It's a helpful technique for empowering you to identify the barriers that stand in your way of having what you say you want in relation to money.

Take a few moments to write down your answer to the following questions. I've included examples of possible answers in *italics*, but this exploration will be most valuable to and enjoyable by brainstorming all of your own truths and not mine. Be as articulate as possible. The more information you provide the more clear you will be in revealing your context and personal limitations around money. It's great to do this with a friend or partner too. These are questions a good coach would ask of you. I use them with clients all the time.

1. What is true about money? What are your judgments, beliefs, opinions, assumptions and expectations about money? Include your superficial thoughts about money as well as your core truths about money.

   Examples:

   - Money creates pain for people who have it and for people who don't have it.

   - I will never have enough money.

   - You have to work hard to get enough money

   - I believe I can generate all the money I want.

   - Money is the root of all evil.

   - The more money you have the more responsible you have to be.

   List a minimum of 15 of your truths about money.

2. Based on what is true for you, what actions do you take regarding money? These actions can sometimes compensate for what is true, while others can support your truth positively.

Examples:

- I worry and feel anxious that I will never have enough money.
- I make as little money as possible so I can avoid the pain of losing it.
- I play the stock market for fun and for profit.
- I balance my checkbook so I always know how much I have in my bank account.
- Every month I give money to charity because I know there's always more than enough for me.

Notice in the examples listed above that actions include thinking and feeling, as well as specific behaviors we take. Again, list at least 15 items.

3. When looking at your actions regarding what is true for you about money, what qualities of *being* show up? What does it feel like when looking at the actions you take?

   Examples:

   - I feel ashamed, guilty, anxious and scared.
   - I feel relaxed, excited, prosperous and creative.

   Name the qualities of experience, the felt-sense or feelings that arise. Maybe it's a picture or sound you get instead of a physical response. Whatever response you get, write it down.

4. Looking again at the list of actions you take, to what would you say you are committed?

   Examples:

   - I'm committed to feeling shame and to not risking security for possibility.
   - I'm committed to staying stuck.
   - I'm committed to generosity and prosperity.

Again, base what you are committed on the actions you are taking in relation to your present interpretations about money.

5. Based on this context you have about money (i.e. what is true for you and the actions you take based on what *is* true), what would you say is currently impossible.

   Examples:

   - It's impossible to create prosperity.
   - It's impossible to feel secure.
   - It's impossible to trust myself with money.
   - It's impossible to trust that the Universe will provide.
   - It's impossible to feel loved and worthy enough to have the money I want.
   - It's impossible to take the necessary steps to create the prosperity I really want.
   - It's impossible to trust that my money won't disappear.

6. What would it be like if what is currently impossible became possible? Imagine you are creating prosperity. What does it look like or feel like? What is the quality of the experience of having the impossible be possible? This exercise is most powerful when you can stay in the present tense as opposed to future tense.

   Examples:

   - I feel relaxed, strong, capable and energized.
   - I feel expansive, at ease, playful and spontaneous.
   - I feel freedom and fun.
   - I feel trusting.

- I see myself on a beach having fun and enjoying my family.

This is an exercise in having you feel the physicality of the experience. Sometimes it's challenging to bring your awareness into your body, but this is where all of our sensations and feelings reside. All emotions come through our physical body. It is a vast resource from which to tap.

7. From a place of being *relaxed, strong, capable* and *energized* (whichever word(s) you used above), what is true for you about money?

   Examples:

   - What is true about money from a place of being relaxed, strong, capable and energized is that I can make all the money I want.
   - There is more than enough.
   - I haven't any reason to feel insecure or worry about risk.
   - Money isn't a painful subject.

8. What actions can you take coming from this new set of truths?

   Examples:

   - I will be relaxed, live more in faith, act more responsibly with my money and be more proactive with my investing.
   - I will take more time off work in order to enjoy more freedom and balance in my life, knowing I have what I need to make the money I want.

What have you noticed through this exploration about yourself, your interpretations and your power to create? My intention for providing this exercise is that you notice it's just a matter of shifting how you are *being* in relation to money. By shifting how you are *being*, you shift your beliefs, interpretations, expectations, judgments and assumptions. What comes next, if you choose, is to practice *being* to allow these new interpretations and actions to permeate your everyday life.

"All right," I hear you say now, "but I'm afraid." This is where you get to practice living in faith.

Faith

Faith is the most powerful tool for changing everything you want to change in your life. The practice of faith supports you in changing this invisible vibrational field about which both scientists and spiritual experts talk.

As with our beliefs about power, success, politics or religion, we are extremely reluctant to loosen our grip on our beliefs about money, regardless that so many of our beliefs hold no evidence of truth and provide no support for what is true in relation to money. We are stuck in our beliefs because of our context and our way of *being* tied into that context.

I can point to the time in my life when I was on welfare. I can point to the time when I was in school and couldn't afford to pay my rent or pay my student loan once I completed school. I can point to how I struggled to have enough money well into my fifties; however, if I look at my context, list the truths I had about money at that time and the actions I took in relation to what was true, I see my beliefs and actions actually created the circumstances as evidence to support my truth.

The practice of faith only requires you to begin to consider the possibility that it could be different. If this is easy, choose a different way of *being* in relation to money and practice that for just five minutes. This is a practice of faith. This is easy. Practice it for a day, a week, a month. Your willingness to be with something new without knowing what will unfold is the practice of faith.

A Case in Point

I was in my thirties at a time when I was on welfare. I read a book by Jane Roberts called, *The Nature of Personal Reality: A Seth Book.* It was the most life-changing book I had ever read. Among much of the wisdom found within, I came across the fundamental point of the book, which is the idea that we create our reality by choosing our beliefs. As an exercise, it said to list your beliefs around a particular subject. Since I was in a state of poverty, I worked with that. As I listed my particular beliefs, I could see I was creating this particular situation of being on welfare to punish my parents for being unavailable in ways

I needed them most. (My belief was, if I were unsuccessful in my life, my parents would have to accept that they were crumby parents).

I created this poverty to avoid feeling guilty for choosing to give custody of my children to their father because of his financial stability and my need to create a resourceful life for myself and my children. (My belief was, if I was successful financially, it would be to the detriment of my children and I felt guilty about that). One other belief I had was, if I were broke, someone would come and rescue me.

The fact is; regardless of the financial crisis I created for myself, my parents continued to be detached from my circumstances and me. They didn't appear to be fazed one bit by my being on welfare. They weren't feeling punished at all. They were off having a great life and my children were getting the short end of the stick by my being on welfare. I couldn't visit them or have them visit me because I had so little money. I couldn't afford to send them gifts to let them know I was thinking of them.

It became clear very quickly that what I had chosen to believe wasn't working for me. It didn't take me long to realize that if I chose those particular beliefs then I could choose different beliefs. I decided to give up the idea I could punish my parents and I started living my life for myself. I also decided I wanted to have more time with my children and be able to provide them with gifts when I wanted. Within weeks of my choosing to decide differently, my financial circumstances turned around and within two months, I had a full-time job doing the work I was trained to do as a marriage and family therapist.

So, what became clear for me then and continues to become clearer is that it's not about the circumstances. It's my beliefs about my circumstances, money and my parents. My thoughts, interpretations, beliefs and expectations all form the way I am *being* and the actions I take toward my circumstances and the people and things therein.

Through the process of revealing specific unconscious beliefs there has been a continual unraveling of unconscious perceptions that create my reality. As I live more in courage and faith, I have more potential to reveal my *truths* and change them to be in alignment more with my higher self and my higher truths.

COACHING QUESTIONS: *List the beliefs you have around money. What was it that had you create these particular beliefs? How are these beliefs serving you? Are your beliefs about money in alignment with your highest truth and your highest purpose? Are you willing to shift your beliefs, just as a practice, to see what might show up? What are some new beliefs you would consider taking on?*

If you can shift your beliefs about money, you can shift your beliefs about anything!

What Would You Have to Give Up in Order to Shift Your Beliefs About Money

You may have noticed there's nothing to give up and there's no suffering by doing the context exercise above. You choose how you want to be in relation to money. You can see that how you are *being* supports your decision and the circumstances that follow. Change how you are *being* and your beliefs transform because your perceptions, view and lenses change. It's a valuable practice to notice not only your beliefs, but also notice for what you are looking.

Steven Covey's *Seven Habits of Highly Effective People* reveals that successful people make choices based on values. They prioritize their values and they prioritize their projects to support their values. We do this unconsciously all of the time! In the context exercise, we revealed the actions we take based on what's true about money. Then asked, based on those actions, to what would you say you are committed? It isn't at all uncommon to have people say they are committed to saying safe, looking good, avoiding risk and staying stuck. Most of us are committed to avoiding risk and playing it safe, though it isn't spoken aloud often. Staying safe by avoiding risk is a value. As long as this is at the top of your list, you will find the changes you want in your life won't occur or will very sssllooowwwlllyyy! Change takes place rarely through avoiding risks and staying safe.

When clients tell me they are committed to having more money in their lives, I listen for how they relate to themselves around money. I don't listen so much to what they say they are committed, but I pay attention to what they are doing in the present. I am curious about which value is being served by their way of *being* with money.

COACHING QUESTIONS: *What is it you want in relation to money? What values are being served by your present relationship with money? In shifting your relationship with money, which values would be served better? Are you willing to shift how you are being, just for a brief period as a research project, as an investigation or as a practice? Notice also, for what you are looking. Are you looking for evidence to prove you are right about your original beliefs around you and money or are you open to seeing any evidence that supports a potential new belief?*

We started this chapter with the notion that money creates power. What we have discovered though is that money is just money, currency, a form of energy exchange. We revealed that we add significance, meaning, interpretations, *truth* and evidence of that *truth* and how we *be* with that *truth.* All of this creates possibility and limits possibility. We revealed, additionally that we are at choice about what we choose to believe and how to be with that choice.

As you explore what's true for you, enjoy the process. See what's possible. You may find yourself exploring many other relationships using these tools. Regardless of the context, you will find that your interpretations and your beliefs form the foundations of what is showing up in your life, what is creating possibility and what is presently impossible. Have fun!

Practice Areas

- Consider making a plan for financial success. List all of the processes incorporated in creating that success such as a budget, savings account, investments or an IRA.
- Notice what shows up immediately in your considerations. What do you experience physically and emotionally? What thoughts or feelings, anxiety or discomforts arise?
- Notice what you want to do with these feelings and sensations. What do you want to do to avoid, distract or deny your present experience? Are these actions taking you closer to your financial goals or away from them?

  This is where most people will close the book, flip to the next chapter or take a nap. This is the moment where most of us live into our commitment to remain the same and avoid possibility. If you are like most of us, you will stop right here and miss the opportunity to experience what is beyond your self-limiting behaviors. It's up to you!

- Consider the practice of making another financial plan. Notice again, what shows up.
- Ask yourself if there are other options as you respond to the financial plan you just considered.
- Repeat this process, noticing resistances, rationalizations and justifications for not following through.
- Notice too, it's not about the money. It's *never* about the money.

The Truth

The Truth
Is such a Lover
She ruins you
For anyone else

To fly
Is to have Her
Under your wings
There isn't enough muscle
In your wing
To fly without Her

With Her
We surrender to "what is"
And we are given back
Our freedom

Freedom from what?
Freedom from
The mind's tyranny
Over the Heart

Truth is:
Non-resistance to what is
Chris McCombs, August 5, 2007

Chapter 4: Relationship to (Im)possibility

My client Rick has a truly amazing relationship to *impossibility.* This man has done the impossible, not once, not twice, but many times. Some of it wasn't pretty. In fact, there are aspects of his life that were darn near ugly.

By the time Rick was 15, he was a practicing alcoholic and drug addict who lived in Texas. He became clean and sober and created a career for himself in alcohol and drug rehabilitation by the time he was 20. He was loved and respected for his capacity to support individuals in their recovery.

When he was 22, Rick sat with a loaded gun in his mouth for an hour and a half; waiting for that magic moment when he would pull the trigger and leave this world forever. That moment didn't come.

On a whim, at 24 and motivated by the desire to become an actor, he moved from his hometown in Texas to Los Angeles with seven dollars in his pocket. He turned his life around. Though he has yet to become an actor, he worked successfully in television for nine years and made hundreds of thousands of dollars. When he realized that his life was less than satisfying and meaningful in the television business, he took a sabbatical to figure out what was next for him.

He met his wife, Beth near the end of 1998. They worked together all day and every day. For three years, they were platonic coworkers who loved each other madly, but had incompatible sexual orientations and the accompanying partners. Six years ago, they had a clandestine affair that lasted one year. In February of 2002, Rick told his spouse and Beth told her partner of the affair. They left their significant others and moved in together. In June of 2005, they flew to Hawaii and had a small and beautiful wedding.

A few months after their marriage, fourteen hours before surgery for thyroid cancer and because of a conversation with a naturopathic physician, Rick took himself off the list of procedures to be done at a hospital and over a matter of months, cured himself of cancer.

As amazing as Rick's life appears, he is caught in a trap that feels hopeless, paralyzing and impossible to change. His anguish and pain brought him to request support through coaching.

Here's what the impossible looks like today; his relationship with work, money and personal power is extremely unsatisfying. He feels stuck and incapable of making a difference in his life. He overspends, is overstressed and has a self-sabotaging practice manifesting as a salary that doesn't cover the bills. He is in crisis mode and wants to shift his relationship to all of this that presently seems impossible.

Even though Rick's life has been filled with many blessings and miracles, he has been caught in this dynamic all his life. It's all been covered up by many beliefs and ideas he's had about himself that oddly enough, had him feel good about himself while feeling bad.

The first step out of this predicament for Rick was to begin working with a financial counselor, reorganize his debt payment plan and begin his financial life anew. This strategy took care of his present financial circumstance, but not the underlying beliefs and interpretations that contributed to and supported the imbalance of his circumstances. Rick has created a multilayered and deliciously rich set of strategies and over the first eight weeks that we worked together, he has revealed them one at a time. Listed below are some of the themes that contributed to Rick appearing paralyzed, hopeless and helpless:

- The safety of romancing, "Surviving is romantic... Eking out a living is romantic, as is being acted upon by external circumstances. Struggle, martyrdom, wishing and hoping are all romantic to me... Feeble is more romantic than self-righteousness, anything is romantic... Unrequited, unfulfilled, unconsummated longing... Pining—the promise of unrealized potential, somehow is much more romantic than realized potential. I almost died many times. There's beauty in it as I talk about it... Tragic, dismalness in the failure. It's romantic in refusing this imposed destiny of artist and brilliance... All that, without seeing that I am actually choosing nothing and feeling so isolated."
- Safety in living the layaway plan, "Don't enjoy what I'm doing now so I can enjoy myself later. Just keep longing for those days to come when..."
- The safety of the dream, "It's so much safer to imagine and dream where the outcome is certain. My dad was a dreamer to the core, a tragic romantic.

He always taught me to dream. I thought this was a good thing, but I get now that dreaming keeps me from doing and being in my life in the present instead of futurizing."

- The safety of, "I could never do that… I'm too young, I'm too old, I'm too smart, I'm too dumb or it's too late for me."
- The safety of self-denial, "It's noble to deny myself stuff. I get to look generous, caring and loving."
- The safety of self-righteous inaction, "I get to believe that I'm better than others as long as I don't do anything where I have to prove that I'm not."
- The safety of telling stories about my life, "I'm great at telling people the big stories of my life, the cancer, my divorce and my meeting Beth. I see that I tell the exact story with the same inflection every time. I get something from this. Constructed and told the same way every single time. I'm deciding whom you see me as and controlling that—here is me, the one I will let you know. It's a dusty, rotting idea of who I am: smart, funny and charismatic. I don't show you that I'm a broke, frustrated, romantic and noble dreamer. I show you that I am a heroic figure who has overcome the impossible by living a simple life. What it is, is a genuine and contrived well-constructed story of overcoming the impossible. Who am I without *the story*?"
- The safety of managing brilliance instead of living a brilliant life, "My duty to my parents and family was to realize my potential, but their expectation of me did not feel good. Who am I to claim my brilliance? Always having to manage the arrogance of being brilliant… I had to maintain constant vigilance to keep me from coming across as an arrogant know-it-all. I got power in refusing to live up to my anticipated potential."
- The safety of false humility, "I find false humility more attractive than confidence. I pretend to be small for the sake of having people like me, not risking falling on my face, being a failure, fear of not being as big as I think I am."

As safe as Rick has made his life and as rich as the internal environment that surrounds him, due to the qualities of romance and fantasy, he still feels like a loser. He likes that he looks good as a loser, but this façade is wearing thin. He sees through his own illusion and it sickens him.

Rick's strategies are beginning to break down. Grief and anger are beginning to surface; a sure sign he is awakening. "I feel sad about the not knowing and about the fear… about my neglecting to take care of myself in a better way. Twenty years ago, I chose to do this work, but within the first five years in LA, I became stagnant. My awakening became uncomfortable and I slowed down. What that did to my first wife and my life! It cost me a lot! My divorce was a wake-up call. I got into therapy and started to become conscious. I didn't want to sleepwalk anymore, but the truth is that I continue to drag my feet."

Rick is an amazing role model for making the impossible possible and he is on that precipice yet again. Though he doesn't want to sleepwalk anymore, he is still very much attached to his ideas and identifications that keep him from having the life he says he wants. He has demonstrated numerous times in his life that he can create the impossible. Can he do it again and create a life worth living?

Making the Impossible Possible

Like Rick, we all imagine ourselves in the most wonderful, amazing and perhaps even exotic circumstances. How many of our imaginings are real enough to realize? Which ones do we discredit as outlandish and impossible? How much of our time is spent envisioning that *we can't* in order to maintain the dream, the illusion of how we want to be seen. How much of our time do we spend daydreaming instead of taking action toward that which we say we want and yet, how much time do we spend thinking of these dreams as if they are never going to happen? In fact, what's the point of taking any action on something that we see to be impossible? There has to be some rationale to our desire or we will never take action. Just thinking something is impossible creates resistance to thinking differently and making it possible.

Sometimes it is a matter of just pushing through your resistance. In fact, it is a huge part of any regimen; to exercise muscles of determination, discipline and just plain doing it, but there is an easier way to relax that, which is creating the resistance. ***Get clear that your resistance is fueled by some belief or decision you made about yourself, the world or that which you say you want.*** By unconcealing the belief that is creating the resistance, you are then at choice to shift the belief to something that is empowering. This process allows you to have what you say you want with ease and effortlessness, even if it seems impossible.

Rick's push to release himself from his powerful identifications and interpretations in order to have the life he wants is making a difference. The stories and illusions are disappearing and yet, he is still unsure of who he is. It's an anxious time; however, through the exploration, he continues to experience glimmers of hope. He's revealing more of his shtick; "I'm, out to prove I'm not like them: resigned, mediocre and regular. I have to give up the 'look how great I am' if I'm going to really live from my authentic self." Rick is moments away from popping through his attachment to these illusions and the resistance that ensues. Every time he chooses to reveal more of his illusional interpretations, the closer he comes to choosing his unadulterated and authentic self. This is all in the service of making the impossible possible.

Because You Say So

Your dream is only possible because you say so and it's only impossible because you say so.

At what point do you shrug your shoulders, give up and walk away from the fight for the most exceptional life ever lived? Big question! This is the choice-point that Rick is at presently.

What does it take you to take a stand for yourself, your career or for your life, only because you say so? No 'yes, buts' allowed. No excuses. No justifications. No rationalizations and no logical explanations. It is just because you say so.

I'm sure you have heard many miraculous stories, like Rick's, of people healing themselves from incurable diseases, money falling from the sky or about people finding the love of their lives at age 72. There are so many stories about people who have experienced the impossible, just because they said it was possible. We don't need to discuss all of the impossible inventions that have come into reality just because someone knew it could be done. Life on this planet is miraculous and full of impossibilities that turn not only into possibilities, but also into reality.

As a life coach, I want my clients to reach for the impossible. I want them to experience the desire and the fulfillment that comes with attaining what only feels like a dream. I want them to reveal and eliminate any obstacle in the way of creating something beyond their wildest dreams. I want them to understand it is essential to allow the wanting and allow the vulnerability that comes with wanting. This is what I want for you, too.

I also want my clients to distinguish the impossible from fantasies, which ones are probable and which ones are beyond improbable. It is not my job to tell a client, which is which. My job is to empower them to empower themselves so they can live into their dreams and desires and bring them into manifestation. I want them to see how they may be using their fantasies to avoid living into their dreams. Sometimes there is a fine distinction between fantasy and impossible dreams. It's through the process of inquiry and distinguishing that one realizes which one is which.

The intention of this chapter is to distinguish the impossible from the possible and show what makes the difference. Much like we did with Rick, we will decode particular beliefs and interpretations that interfere with manifesting the life you want. We will investigate the real hostage taker, the one that sabotages any expression completely beyond the edge of your comfort zone—fear of failure. We will explore our stand for invulnerability that limits our willingness to reach beyond our safety zone. We will also investigate hope, faith and knowing as traveling companions. What we are after is empowering yourself to be with what confronts you most.

What Is Impossible

One of my favorite prints of all times is by Quint Buchholz called *Giacomond*, meaning *The Edge*. It shows a man walking a tightrope with moonlight illuminating his way across the evening sky. One end of the rope is attached to the edge of a rooftop many feet behind him. The other end of the rope is in his left hand. He is walking out beyond the known and the possible. His posture denotes confidence and clarity of intention. There appears to be great peril in his endeavor yet, in his demeanor there is an essence of calm-presence and ease. He doesn't press forward in his conviction, he doesn't struggle with effort and he has no fear. The print denotes the impossible occurring effortlessly. My experience is that it is effortless, more often than not, when we allow ourselves full empowerment to make it so.

Impossibility is common among those who say it can't be done. On the other hand, scientists and inventors all over the world are creating the unimaginable because they believe nothing is impossible. We live in a world that is full of things that seemed impossible a hundred years ago. It was the rare individual who dreamed such possibilities and envisioned technologies we take for granted now. The creation of the impossible is happening faster than ever before. Jerry and Esther Hicks, in *The Amazing Power of Deliberate Intent* say, "If you can think it, you can create it."

I suggest, for the remainder of this chapter, you practice using the following phrase to support the manifestation of your desires, ***"It's possible only because I say so."***

Fantasy and Impossibility on the Way to Self-Empowerment

I used to be a daydreamer, especially in my youth. I would lose myself in a world where I was safe, loved and valued for just being me. I could play freely, openly and just be a kid in this dream. Given the environment in which I lived, this was just a fantasy; it was impossible to change any of my real life circumstances in order for me to have what was available in my fantasies. I did not have the tools, skills or resources to make possible what I wanted desperately and found available in my daydreams.

In my real life, I chose to give up self-dignity for belonging and surviving, though both felt shallow, unfulfilling and meaningless. I gave up self-wisdom and self-knowledge for the security of not being left, rejected or abandoned. I settled for the American dream and gave up the American way of innovation, self-reliance and independence. I believed it to be impossible to have dignity, self-love and belonging at the same time. This took me to the edge of suicide many times. Ending my life became a possibility, but never a probability.

As I grew older, matured and became more capable, I gained access to tools and resources that allowed me to have what it was I wanted. With conviction, commitment and practice, over time I created a life that allows playful abandon, self-love and creativity. What made the difference? I empowered myself to access what I needed to create what had been an impossibility.

It wasn't just a matter of growing up. It was that I found resources and people who believed in me and saw me for who I was, trusted me and enjoyed me. I also found something within myself. I found the courage to find out who I am beyond my limited beliefs of that which I should be, how I should be and what I should be. I was willing to risk being unlovable and rejected by people to whom I'd given my power. I risked taking my power back, risked making mistakes and failure for the sole purpose of finding what was true for me. A lot of that was sorting through beliefs and assumptions that no longer served me in order to find what did serve me.

Many steps of this journey felt impossible. I had limited financial resources and little emotional support from my family and friends. It was a matter of taking it one-step-at-a-time. It didn't matter how slow my progress, it didn't matter the outcome; I was discovering who I was as I explored and expanded my capacity for self-love, *self-realization* and self-respect.

During my time of being on welfare and in an abusive relationship, my life seemed really off track. I decided to give up my belief of what was impossible and I began to create what was possible through a moment-by-moment process. I began creating a life one-step-at-a-time. I would ask myself, "What is possible in this moment?" Then, "What is possible in this moment," and then, "What is possible in this moment..."

The resources that had not been available when I saw my dream as impossible now appeared more frequently and easily as I began to live, think and feel differently. I exposed myself to ways of being that had been out of my known reality, beyond doing and succeeding as I had been doing. I practiced surrendering my will, as they say in twelve-step programs, to a power greater than myself. That no longer meant giving over my personal power to someone who did not honor or respect me. It meant changing the things I could change and surrendering my control when I couldn't.

During this time, I began to learn through experience, what faith really means. I was learning that true power is available by being vulnerable and humble. Finding more peace and gratitude, I began giving up my self-righteousness and manipulative behavior gradually.

Vulnerability: Why Would Anyone Be Afraid of Being Vulnerable

Living on the cutting edge of your life requires living in your personal power and being vulnerable at the same time. Shifting your context around vulnerability is required, as is shifting your context around personal power.

It's one thing to be children, vulnerable to attacks and rejection from parents, siblings and strangers over whom you have no control. It is another to choose to face what is currently present in your life as an adult; unsure of the outcome, but damn sure you have the personal power to be with what is.

My friend Ko called this morning. "Hi, I'm feeling vulnerable," she says to me in a tone of voice that emanates weakness and helplessness. "Good for you. That's a good thing," I say in return. She can't help herself and laughs at my nonchalant response to what she thinks to be a frail and defenseless experience. "Why would anyone be afraid of being vulnerable?" She quips back at me. The humor in the moment breaks the tension and helps Ko be with her fear, worry, anxiety and isolation.

Ko grew up as a single child, adopted by parents who loved her dearly; however, they were alcoholic, abusive and angry people. Ko was vulnerable to emotional and physical abuse from a very early age. She, like all of us as children, learned ways of being invulnerable in order to protect her heart while being attacked and to avoid further attacks. The strategies she developed: being cute, funny, and street-smart and always in, protected her from disappointments, rejection and betrayal, but they didn't stop the wounding; they just anesthetized the pain.

Over the past few decades, Ko has come to realize that she's created a community of people who love her and with whom she feels safe. She is practicing being vulnerable now, with less need to protect and defend. More often, she is finding herself safe in the midst of potential abandonment that surfaces with every new relationship she begins. Ko's next step is to allow herself to be vulnerable to what is presently in her life, taking the shields of control and manipulation down and just being authentic and raw with what is.

Learning to Be Invulnerable

At age six, while on the jungle gym at elementary school, Jocelyn said to her friend, "I gotta get out of this town. There aren't enough smart people here." As a child, she witnessed grownups being insensitive, inconsiderate and untrustworthy, lacking respect and being unaccountable for their actions. They would break promises, lie and be anything, but present to their children. Like Ko, to protect herself, Jocelyn became invulnerable to this display of inhumanity by becoming intolerant. She blocked out the pain of disenchantment by judging people as being less than and at this very early age, in her mind, took the higher ground. Even as a very young girl, she prided herself on her wisdom and intellect, and focused her intentions on becoming even more intelligent, conscious and caring to avoid the pitfalls into which most adults fall.

Now, a brilliant and charismatic woman in her forties, Jocelyn is known for her brutal honesty and her lack of tolerance for people who are, in Jocelyn's words, *"dim-witted, stupid, slow and unaccountable."* She was known as the *go-to* person, in her office, if you wanted a clear and unadulterated critique of your work.

Today, Jocelyn is facing an interesting challenge. She is taking on a career as a life and business coach. In this field, intolerance will not get her very far. In one of our supervision sessions, Jocelyn worked a particular issue she was having with a client. This client was from Italy and her English was far from perfect. She would often ramble on, seeming to be unconscious of what she was actually saying. Jocelyn shared with me, "She talked just to hear herself talk." From Jocelyn's perspective, this client hadn't the capacity for meaningful, deliberate conversation to the degree in which Jocelyn was familiar. The result was Jocelyn became frustrated, angered and intolerant of this client. Though her client never knew, Jocelyn couldn't wait to have their coaching agreement over.

Jocelyn is at a choice-point. She has been using her winning strategies of being brilliant, astute, judicious and invulnerable, while at the same time, underutilizing strategies that are within her experience and have been available to her. While visiting other cultures, Jocelyn allows herself access to strategies like patience, allowing and fascination. She enjoys the adventure of the not knowing. The funny thing is that while she is traveling, she feels no *vulnerability* and no need to create invulnerability, but within the coaching session, the thought of letting go of her strategy of intolerance has her feeling as if she is *out in the desert with no tools to find water.* Interesting! What element creates fears and risks in one environment and fearlessness in another?

Vulnerability is not a word that suggests safety, strength and courage; however, if you face the impossible task of unfolding your life to its highest potential, you will undoubtedly face peril and the danger of ridicule, rejection and failure. You will be vulnerable to attack, but you do this already and all the time. You take risks and agree to be vulnerable whenever you want something bad enough. They are calculated risks; nonetheless, they *are* risks.

COACHING QUESTIONS: *Think about some choices you have made in your life: quitting school, moving to a new state, getting a job, starting new relationships or beginning a new health practice. Each choice requires a level of vulnerability. You had to and were willing to be vulnerable for the sake of having what you wanted. What values did you want to serve enough so that you would choose to be vulnerable? What did you value more than safety? To what degree were you committed to what you said you wanted? What were you willing to risk to have that which you said you wanted? What did you have to give up?*

What Is Required

What is required of you to create the impossible?

- You must have enough life experience to provide you with the evidence that you have the capacity to survive, succeed and triumph over adversity. If you are reading this, you have passed through this portal of impossibility.
- You have to be willing to acknowledge that you created and adopted strategies to ensure your survival through circumstances you could not avoid (childhood, the educational system, social situations, religion, etc.). You chose ways to be invulnerable in order to survive. Good job!
- You have to be willing to notice strategies that continue to keep you invulnerable, safe and risk-free to circumstances that require a different level of presence, openness and vulnerability ***only if you want a different outcome.***
- You have to be willing to practice opening and allowing new ways of being with your present circumstances. This can be done at your own pace. Take your time! There is no hurry and no time limit.
- You have to be willing to acknowledge you for *being* with these new practices successfully and for being with the changes that are occurring.
- You have to continue to practice opening and allowing possibility to be present in your life and open to experiencing the vulnerability that comes along with it.
- You have to be willing to experience the excitement and the exhilaration of creating something new, paying attention to your body's response when you empower yourself and the success that follows from that practice.

If you choose to choose invulnerability, if you choose to choose the same actions that reinforce invulnerability in order to get what you say you want, then it is certain that you will fail to have what you say you want. It is crucial that you understand this is not failure on your part. You are failing to *choose* differently and at the same time, you are succeeding at having it *be* the same as before. You are *choosing* to have it the same as it always was. You are *choosing* not to have what you say you want. This is not failure.

Using failure as a *justification* for remaining invulnerable and avoiding risk minimizes your capacity to empower yourself, to be on purpose, and to be fulfilled. You are getting ever closer to that which you say you want. My hope is that you will empower yourself sooner, rather than later, to bring about the shifts that will allow you to know just how magnificent and powerful you are. Eventually you will make the choice.

Fear of Success

We touched on this briefly in an earlier chapter—people facing their future, dreams and desires often face fear of success and failure. Many people avoid success in order to avoid certain levels of responsibilities, but avoiding success in order to avoid responsibility is not the same as failing. It is *choosing* to choose something other than that level of success and that level of responsibility that comes along with it. They are choosing a level of success that allows a certain amount of responsibility, which may allow them to be more relaxed and less stressed. The conversation can look and feel like failure, but it's not.

Making excuses, justifying and rationalizing or not following through with actions that will get you what you say you want, in order to avoid success, is not failure. It is choosing to choose something other than that level of success. *Being at choice about how you want to be with success is success. Failure to be at choice, failure to be responsible and accountable to your dreams and visions, will have success look and feel like failure.* There is no such thing as failing to succeed. Many of us are masterful at succeeding to fail. In fact, the many strategies put to use in having us fail, are the very strategies that are useful in succeeding at getting what we say we want. Again, interesting!

It may be easier to acknowledge what is true, rather than creating a façade of trying and failing. It's being clear about what you want. Someone might say, "I would like to be an airplane pilot and fly those jumbo jets, but I don't want the responsibility of all the passengers that would fly with me. I'm happy just imagining myself as a pilot." This is being honest. With this level of honesty comes empowerment to create with authenticity and accountability. Just consider the possibilities!

Yalon

Yesterday, I had my first session with an amazing man. Yalon is 38 years old and in the higher echelon of one of the top computer companies in the world. He has been in this particular career for over 14 years and he has realized that there is very little enjoyment for him in his work. When he wakes up in the morning, the thought of going to work does not inspire or motivate him to get out of bed. The money is good, he knows how to do what needs to be done, but it isn't satisfying his need for meaning and fulfillment.

We talked about what he wanted concerning a new career and together we were able to distinguish quickly what he wanted. What became clear is that Yalon enjoys the process of innovative thinking. Creative problem solving inspires him and when he has a good team to take his ideas and run with them, he is thrilled to go to work; however, this is only part of his present job. The rest of it is very mundane and unimportant to him.

Both an individual just coming out of school, preparing to open their first private practice or one holding a high executive position with many years in the field, will encounter this particular same moment. Each one of us, considering something new, faces the potential for success and failure. Pulling back when reaching the edge of possibility is common and Yalon is no exception.

When doing career coaching, I quickly step into the conversation about failure. I want to get it out of the way in order to reveal the individual's willingness to risk failure for a life worth getting out of bed. I don't want to be two or three months into the work to find that fear of failure is sabotaging our progress and my client's dream.

In our first session, I want to know whether the Yalon is willing to be with the potential of failure in such a way that allows him access to all of the talents and gifts he has to share. Will he choose to be vulnerable and take risks for the sake of realizing his dream?

"What will stop you from making the shift to something new?" I asked Yalon.

"What stopped me all of these years are three things: one is the fear of failure, two is my concern for what people think of me and three is my lack of confidence. As a child, I had it rough. I was unsuccessful at school and the brunt of jokes. I learned to survive by being what others wanted of me. I looked for any indication of acceptance and just kept doing that over and over again." He was very clear in his response because he had thought about this for a very long time.

Yalon chose very early in life to abandon his *authentic self* and look to others for his better reflection. He mentioned this numerous times, indicating that he was somehow flawed and because of this, he would fail to succeed. He felt this flaw limited his ability to move ahead in his life in relation to fulfillment. If he is more concerned with what other people think, will he ever allow himself to follow his own heart and passion? This is a place where Yalon disempowers himself and for a man who has created so much material success, it was important to give him a new perspective on this flaw and as quickly as possible.

Through inquiry, Yalon was able to reframe this *flaw*, this need for approval, as an effective strategy in which he engaged early in life in order to feel connected, important and loved and to avoid rejection, ridicule, humiliation, and shame. He understood how this is a very important skill for all children to develop. Each child needs to find their own level of connection and belonging and their own strategies for building relationships. This is an essential set of tools and most of us, like Yalon, have learned to rely on our ability to be outer-directed looking outside ourselves for validation of worth. Others are more inner-directed and get their sense of self-worth from themselves. It is good to have a balanced outlook, sometimes seeking validation from the outside world while other times finding it from within. For Yalon, he became dependent on seeking approval solely from others, thus avoiding physical and emotional abuse, but also losing connection with his core self—his truth.

Yalon was able to hear himself in such a way that engaged him deeper in the conversation. He was discovering that what he carried as a wound and disability was now something he could see as a strategy for creating an identity, one that allowed him to take care of himself, perhaps through the only vehicle open to him. We, like Yalon, employ whatever it takes to avoid rejection, humiliation, criticism and personal failure. This is required for the survival of our spirit.

I saw a softening and an opening. I read in his eyes that perhaps there was hope for him; not for the adult, but for the child who long ago developed specific strategies not to be seen for the failure he assumed himself to be. He could now allow the experience of possibility to emerge. He could claim his authentic self beyond the façade he had taken on. This aspect of Yalon was hidden for decades and probably would have remained hidden, impossible to disclose or reclaim. I believe without this opening, it would have been impossible for him to risk vulnerability and fulfill his sense of purpose.

What Yalon knows is that the aspect of his self that created the strategies also allows him a certain level of success in his career, but this strategizing-self cannot feel the fulfillment and soulful depths reached only through his authentic being. As the innocent child-self, he experienced failure to be liked, acknowledged and valued. What possibility can there be for this man to rise fully to a position of soul-full and fulfilled living? Risk must be taken. He must risk finding out that he *isn't* enough.

With his capacity as a child, given his culture, religion, gender, family and status, Yalon's innocent-self wasn't capable of making it in this world; although, he does have evidence that the modified self, the self that created strategies for success, can make it happen.

Like a big brother, his strategic-self protected Yalon's innocent-self; however, it's not enough. The strategic-self is capable of managing circumstances in the word, but it is not capable of thriving soulfully because it is not the real self. It's an artificial self, one created to meet circumstances in the world.

In *Star Trek: The Next Generation*, the android, Data was developed to serve humans beyond their competence and ability. He had many human qualities and capabilities, but he did not have the capability to feel emotions. Like Data, the strategic self thrives in the material world, with the potential to achieve a high-level of success; however, it cannot thrive from a heartfelt place. Only the authentic human self has the capacity to experience this deeper soulful satisfaction.

Here is the dilemma for Yalon, he can continue to use the same strategies that manage and control his life and avoid risk and vulnerability or he can be open to exploring his capacity to include more of his authentic self, risking exposure and vulnerability. This dilemma is one we all face many times throughout life.

Sometimes, a big brother can lose sight of his original intention to protect and he can begin to control out of righteousness and a false sense of power. He can forget that he started out protecting something or someone and begin protecting himself. The fear of failure is less significant to him as the strategized self because it knows that it can always find new circumstances in which to play, much as a bully can always find other children to push around.

Consider for a moment that the authentic self can never be abandoned, annihilated or destroyed. It is the essence of our being, our truest nature, universal source, our soul incarnated within our body. It is an aspect of spirit in a sense; it is the organic, unconditioned self. It is real and nothing real can be threatened or destroyed.

As the courageous being that he is, Yalon is stepping into the investigation of this life he's been living. He is curious enough to explore beyond his limiting beliefs and interpretations to see what he once thought to be impossible. He is choosing to take the calculated risks of being vulnerable in order to unconceal a more essential truth lying dormant within his authentic innocence. He is choosing the journey of self-empowerment, self-evaluation and self-remembering. He knows that nothing less will reach and alleviate the exquisite pain of our unexpressed soul, authentic, innocent and non-strategic self.

Six months after our last session, I heard through a mutual friend that Yalon left his position and is taking time paragliding.

Abandoning Hope—The End of Innocence

"This may be as good as it gets." Jack Nicholson in the movie, *As Good As It Gets*

There is a crisis point; a choice point where the innocent self believes it cannot endure within the given circumstances. It suffers a loss of hope and a failure in its ability to hold onto the truth that, "beauty, love and joy are infinite and everywhere and if we just remain open to loving each other, the world would be a wonderful and peaceful place." In this moment, when this innocent being feels the failure to convey and remain in this reality, critical mass is reached and an implosion occurs. I believe this to be the moment when the innocence of our being separates itself from its knowing of its home in Spirit and in God.

At this moment, this being dissociates, creating an amnesiac state forgetting the tranquil state of blissful innocence. For some of us this moment occurs very early and for others, it may occur later. Very few are lucky enough to escape from childhood with their innocence intact.

It is our well-developed mechanisms that will step forward and take charge, choosing methods of operation that allows greater cooperation and survival in the material world. In the book *Exercising Spiritual Intelligence*, I share a moment when, as a six-year-old child and in the first grade at Sacred Heart Church, I abandoned my truth about God, love, joy and acceptance and surrendered my own truth and knowing. I remember clearly the very moment when I decided that the nuns, priests, community and my family must know something I didn't. I capitulated and surrendered in order to survive within a culture that wouldn't have it any other way. I hid the innocent me away and forgot that she ever existed. In my forties, while working on a psycho-spiritual autobiography for my Ph.D., I remembered my innocent self. I reclaimed her. The reunion was exquisite with desperate sobs of remembering.

There is a point at which we come to terms with the fact that we have taken on this physical form and are tied to it for the duration of our time on Earth. Coming to terms with this means, we need to find successful strategies for dealing with this state of being human. In those moments, we dissociate ourselves from the one that cannot survive life's dramas, the one most connected to God or Universal Source/Oneness. We begin very early in life to create personalities that can observe and figure out what strategy will support survival.

None of us escapes childhood without dealing with dilemmas of choosing which strategies will work best for each circumstance. How you relate to your mother and the strategies you use to stay on her good side may be different from those you use to relate with your father, siblings or teachers. You learn to apply your personal strengths to make the most of what you have. My father loved beautiful women; therefore, even in my pre-adolescence, I had enhanced my physical beauty to please him. This did not please my mom—nothing pleased my mom, but at least I could get some attention and acknowledgement from one parent. Based on this observation and practice, I developed a belief that men like beautiful, sexy and available women. To the best of my ability, because my identity was developing around beauty and sex appeal, I focused on being sexy and irresistible to men. It took decades to realize that this never fed my essential requirement to be appreciated for me beyond physical beauty.

By dissociating ourselves from the innocent and failed self and accessing a self that can manage the circumstances and environment in which we are caught, we gain opportunities to expand our repertoire of strategies. We keep doing anything that works. Much of our personalities are just patterns of strategies developed over time. They have become so ingrained that we begin to believe they are real and they become our identity. We live into the possibility of this. Yalon said to me, "I'm a competitive guy. It's my nature." Being competitive is actually a strategy Yalon developed in his career in sales. It's something he developed within his given environment and career demands. Once he gets clear that this is just a strategy to be employed, he will be at choice about the levels of competitiveness that are required or essential for his greater well-being.

The authentic, innocent self has had the experience of complete and utter failure. It knows abandonment, rejection and humiliation. It has experienced annihilation or what felt like annihilation. It knows no way out. It knows what it is like to surrender attempting the impossible and decide never to try again; however, when the pain and suffering are greater than the fear of potential failure, an opening appears perhaps just a crack. In this moment, this concealed, incapacitated failure self begins to consider alternatives. In order to alleviate the pain and discomfort of its confinement, the weakened self initiates the attempt of the impossible. We have waited so long for this moment.

Initially, it takes a great deal of effort and vigilance to disengage from these strategies and the identity we have associated with them. As we cultivate awareness of these strategies and compassion for ourselves ease and effortlessness unfolds. My belief is that mental illness is a deeply ingrained survival mechanism that has most likely saved the lives of those who used them well.

It is my assertion that in the moment, when we choose to dissociate from this state of innocence, we experience a monumental and critical sense of failure, one we never want to repeat. With this failure comes the experience of total and complete annihilation. The Transpersonal Researcher, Stan Grof, revealed in his work that the birth process is actually the first event in this lifetime where we experience the process of annihilation. The trauma of the birth experience is so great that when we get through it and are expelled into the world, we lose all memory of the experience. Our cellular memory carries this experience of trauma for years, perhaps decades and creates similar patterns of trauma throughout our lifetimes until we release the original pattern created at birth. There are various methods for releasing this trauma, all of which go way beyond the parameters of this book; however, they are in service of self-empowerment. Talking with a therapist, breath-work facilitator and various other resources are a value to support you in this process.

Failure

COACHING QUESTIONS: *When you imagine yourself experiencing failure, what is the quality of the experience? When feeling failure what does it feel like in your body? How do you* be *with these qualities and experiences? Do you avoid them, deny them or distract yourself from feeling them? Do you pretend you are fine with them? What strategies do you employ to* deal *with them? From this vantage point, what is impossible for you?*

When striving for success in any domain of your life, the impossible and its companions are nearby. One companion in particular will hound you relentlessly; the fear of failure that you had experienced as an innocent child.

By now you are apt to notice that I love taking concepts and squeezing life into them, singling out the experiences we are loathe wanting from those we wish to have. Failure, the word itself is full of different interpretations; most of which are not at the top of anyone's list of desirable feelings. Each of us has a personal relationship to failure. As you read this, you may be having some visceral and emotional responses. What is the quality of this feeling that you experience in this moment? I propose that the essence of what you are experiencing comes down to feeling resistance and perhaps anxiety. We resist the sensations and feelings of humiliation, shame, rejection, abandonment and the fear of annihilation, all of which are the companions of failure. I will break these into two themes: Abandonment and Rejection or Humiliation and Shame. It's a tossup between the two of which one is the most challenging for you.

For some *humiliation* and *shame* are more challenging. Though both are experienced internally, humiliation and shame are more self-recriminating. The assessment comes more from inside as opposed to fear of rejection, which is a projection of what you fear others will find out or decide about you. Each concept feels uncomfortable, threatening and unsafe. Until you are able to create a greater level of comfort with them, you are destined to create a life within the confines of your fears. This means avoiding events and circumstances that have the potential for failure and avoiding those that may lead you to that which you say you want. Avoiding the circumstance, subject, emotion or experience, limits your ability to create your heart's desire. What I'm suggesting is that you relate to these emotions in a different way. By shifting how you are *being* with them, you allow greater capacity for creating that which you say you want. Let's take a closer look at the feelings and emotions that you don't want to have.

COACHING QUESTIONS: *How do you* be *with feelings of humiliation? How do you* be *with feelings of abandonment? What would have to shift in order to have a different relationship with humiliation or abandonment? If you knew that by shifting your relationship to humiliation and abandonment you could create the life you want, what would you be willing to practice to support this shift?*

Humiliation

Shame and humility go hand in hand. As I allow myself to have the experience of humiliation, I disappear into nothingness and experience annihilation. I feel myself resist avenues of potential success for fear that I may come out looking bad. I'm feeling unworthy. There is emptiness. My skin crawls and I feel uncomfortable. My mind chimes in and the thoughts being, "Writing this book could be a waste of time. I may have wasted years trying to be something I'm not—a writer, an expert and a facilitator of transformation. Maybe I'm none of that. Maybe I have hit my limit, again." I experienced this when I was six years old and the rhetoric in my head continues whenever I try to start something new. The nothingness and emptiness returns; however, as I practice *being with* the experiences and sensations of humiliation and annihilation, I become less resistant to them. I see through the evidence of my life that as many mistakes as I make, I'm still here and I'm healthier and happier than ever. Annihilation has not occurred!

Rejection and Abandonment

Allowing myself to be with the experience of rejection and abandonment reveals another set of responses—I feel disconnected, severed, cut off and isolated. I feel emptiness—a dark void. There is no one or nothing to save me, hold me and make me feel safe. There is despair, anguish, nothing; I am nothing. Doesn't that sound like fun?

Most of us do whatever we can, not to feel these feelings and yet, this is where salvation lies. This is where the impossible becomes possible. Meeting this place, meeting the emotion, the physical sensation as something to be investigated and explored with curiosity and fascination will liberate you from the clutches of a threat that is absolutely false.

Gangaji, an American spiritual teacher of non-dualism, uses a practice of meeting *that, which is perceived as threatening* as a way of empowering individuals to find that there is no substance or truth within that *which feels threatening*. This is a fundamental principle to realizing truth and empowering yourself to manifest your truth.

Each trainee who has completed the Transformational Coaching Training Program and each of my clients, much like Gangaji's devotees, have experienced the process of moving through dislocated, severed and abolished feelings only to find themselves on the other side in a space that feels open, expansive and free. What is available is unlimited potential. They empowered themselves to take the risk and found they were not swallowed or devastated by the experience. They found they were more powerful than their fears and that these fears were mere veils through which they passed effortlessly when approached with curiosity and fascination.

Fear can be paralyzing. It's a great idea to hire a good coach and/or psychotherapist to support you in exercising and strengthening muscles that will empower you to face those fears that have kept you at an impasse. This too may seem impossible, but there are many people who have wonderful and successful lives because they were willing to face what, at first seemed impossible in order to find what was possible.

The future we face is full of potential. Dismantling thoughts and beliefs we've maintained based on the past allows a disintegration of what failure looks and feels like. I noticed a bumper sticker the other day. It read, **"Don't believe everything you think!"**

COACHING QUESTIONS: *Would you be willing to consider that failure doesn't exist at all? What evidence do you have that you are a failure? What are* *some possible ways to reframe your experience of failure? How does it serve you to allow fear of failure to stop you from making the impossible – possible?*

Eliminating Significance: Zero Significance – You Add Meaning

COACHING QUESTIONS: *What is hard for you? (Make a list of at least three things you think are hard.) What makes each of these things hard for you? (Next to each item, write what makes them hard.) What are the thoughts and interpretations that you have when you think of something as hard? What would have to shift to alter your interpretation of this being hard? What is missing, that if it were present, would allow you to let go of the significance to any of these things being so hard?*

In most spiritual traditions, especially the Buddhist traditions, nothing has meaning or significance except for what it is assigned by you. You have a unique interpretation about everything and give each thing a level of significance, value and priority. The level of significance you give something creates your context that dictates what you do, how you do, what you do and how you think and feel about what you do. It also dictates what's possible and what's impossible.

Have you ever been in a kitchen with someone who gives a great deal of significance to doing food preparation in a particular way? Everything has to be done *just so.* We all have that toothpaste-cap thing, toilet paper thing or that driving thing. It is everywhere and in everyone. The *context exercise* we did regarding money was just one area of our lives where we revealed significance. When you distinguish your level of significance around something, you give yourself an opportunity to be at choice about that level and can potentially let go of the significance it had. It alleviates the struggle around many issues and allows possibility to emerge.

When taking on the impossible—*impossible being a relative term*—you can make mountains out of molehills by having huge interpretations about small things. Those who do the impossible make molehills out of mountains by minimizing the significance of the desired outcome.

Richard Carlson said, "Don't sweat the small stuff and it's all small stuff." He was speaking of the idea that we create the hardships, problems and challenges through our perceptions, attitudes and choices to make some things significant. With my clients, I dissuade them from seeing their life, work or desires as hard. It is hard because you say it's hard. I ask them the question, "Would you consider seeing this situation another way?"

Giving something significance gives it a degree of power, value and meaning. Because something has significance to you, it becomes hard, challenging to attain and confronting, and because you have something at stake. We create our whole life, one-day-at-a-time, based on what has meaning and value to us. When you want what you say you want, you create a dilemma. Which thing or experience has more significance; the thing you say you want or what you have already? This dilemma brings you to a *choice-point,* a time to discern what it is you value and how much significance you gave it. If you have given it significance, you can choose differently and give it a different level of significance. You get to decide the level of priority, significance, value, worth and meaning of well… everything. You also get to choose to let go of your attachment to what you want and to what you think of as right, wrong, good or bad. This is one of the most challenging steps to empowering yourself, but one that frees you to manifest the success you want in all your relationships, your career, your spiritual and financial life—all of it.

Now go back and read about Rick in the first part of this chapter. Notice what is significant to him, to what he is attached and where he is stopping himself from emerging from his safe, but an illusional cocoon. You will see how he has created obstacles to an amazing life by holding onto particular ideas as significant. As he becomes more self-empowered, his capacity to release the significance of these notions increases. He loves and desires a romantic life. He loves the idea that he is brilliant, humble and gracious. To have his life turn out the way he wants, he has to give up the significance of these qualities and see what emerges. He is beginning to find that, even though he is letting go, he isn't losing a darn thing.

No Attachment to What You Want

Giving up the attachment to what you say you want doesn't make sense at first glance. Why the heck would you want something if you give up your attachment to having it?

This is why. You won't even take the first step if the attachment to the outcome is so huge and has such significance that it feels too scary. Much as in any recovery process (e.g. Alcoholics Anonymous where "One Step at A Time" is the focus), if we perceive the view as too big, we shrink and resist. Staying present to what needs to occur in this moment is the practice.

COACHING QUESTIONS: *Name some things that you want. List approximately 10 items. Assign each of the items a level of significance based on a scale of zero to 100 where zero represents little to no significance and 100 represents 100% significance. How much do you want it? Are there some items that have a lower level of significance so that if you don't get them, it's all right? What is it that gives one thing more significance to you than another does? How do you decide? What interpretations do you have about that item or about yourself that has you being attached more or less to having what you say you want? What would need to shift for you to lower your level of attachment to any or all of these wants? Would you be willing to consider making these shifts if you knew this would support making the impossible a possibility?*

Through our attachments and the significance we give things, we create resistance and constraint our ability to move freely. Our contexts hold these significances and if we can change our contexts, we can do anything. What does it take?

Hope, Faith and Knowing

In our three-dimensional world, we want to have physical handholds to ensure steadiness and stability thereby, giving us a *sense* of safety. Problem solving supports this condition—If I want to lose 10 pounds I have eat less, exercise more and say my affirmation, "I am losing weight and gaining a beautiful body." We have challenging times when handholds are absent, like the first time you stood on your own two feet and took your first step. No handholds and no safety nets. Something compelling inside you said, "Take the step. You can do it!" and you did take that first step. Using the weight loss analogy, as you are losing weight, there are aspects inside you that want to resist your attempts to have a beautiful body. They have been compelling enough in the past to stop you. This time you are going forward, letting go of the handholds and stepping out beyond your comfort zone.

Just as in the painting, *The Edge* you continually step into your life. You have hope and faith and you have fear. Too many of us live from fear more and from hope and faith less. To create the life you came here to live it is imperative to shift the balance, even just a little, to allow more hope and faith to support you. They are your handholds!

Hope

Hope is one of the most essential experiences in our human existence. We fall into despair without hope for a better day, a better life, a better world—we stop wanting to live—depression and despair would become insurmountable. There is a loss of meaning and a loss of purpose when we don't have hope. However, the flip side of hope can be one of the most useless and paralyzing emotions available to us. We still hope for a turnaround even in the most impossible circumstances. This can be empowering when it allows an opening to possibility, but it is disempowering when it has us avoid or deny responsibility and take action, now!

Hoping can be a pointless practice when it comes to our everyday events, when we use it to avoid personal responsibility for actions taken and for the outcome produced. "I was hoping if I avoided that long enough, it would just go away. I was hoping if I ate just half the number of cookies I usually eat, my diabetes would get better. I was hoping if I said my affirmations every night and every morning, money would come easily." Hope isn't serving the individual in these examples. Hope is used as a strategy to avoid taking responsibility and the required actions for dreams and desires to be realized.

Hope is most ineffective and disempowering when you are looking into the past and hope that things could have been different. In times like these, when you would have liked things to be different, it does no good to hope for a different outcome. Letting go and grieving the loss of the unfulfilled wish may be the last thing you want to do because of the significance you have given it. It's fine not to let go, and it's fine not to want to let go. That's a choice. I want to reveal how each of you creates the impossible by holding on to thoughts and interpretations that no longer serve you. *The choice to maintain hope in a hopeless situation is futile.*

COACHING QUESTIONS: *Notice throughout your day how often you hope your actions will have a different outcome than seems reasonable. "I hope that eating this candy bar won't affect my diabetes." "I hope I won't get a parking ticket even though I've parked my car in a restricted parking zone." Write down how it serves you to act from hope. If you practiced giving up hope, what other potential options are available to you?*

What Have I Got Once I've Abandoned Hope

"I feel hopeless and it feels good. There is surrender in hopelessness. There is quiet and peace yet, a void and I know a safety net is there. I'm safe and I am giving up hope that it will be how I want it to be. I let go of trying to will it in place. I let go of pretending, imagining and efforting to make it happen. I surrender to hopelessness and open myself up to whatever and to everything."~ *Rick*

I believe most of us consider this question at some point in our lives. Choosing to inquire consciously and explore this domain of your life may bring moments filled with sadness, loss and grief; perhaps even terror or memories from your childhood where there was no hope, no way out, no turning left, not turning right—just no turning. The felt-sense of failed attempts returns. It is often the love and respect from a parent, some acknowledgement of our importance, our value and dignity that we hoped would come. When crushed with the disillusionment of our dreams, there is nothing. These memories inform us of what we decided at an earlier time about life, the world and dreams of possibility. What is left is the experience of grief.

Grief

When we abandon hope, I think there is something that feels like devastation, as though we are annihilating our identity, taking us to a place of nonexistence through the portal and process of grief.

When I allow myself the experience of real grief, I feel a total annihilation of my will and a complete loss of control. I no longer have the capability of manipulating events and circumstances that had me believing I could have it my way. I move into a void-like state. I lose the sense of who I am and my connection that which I lose. I'm floating in a bubble, alone and separate. POP!

We're not good at allowing or inviting grief. We will create hope and any other imagined strategy in order to escape the experience of grief; anything to retreat from the edge of what feels like losing our souls.

Once entered though, grief is an exquisite and poignant experience. There are stages of the grief process that include shock, bargaining, anger, depression and resignation; however, the moments of pure grief are most palpable in their capacity to take us through to the better end where we meet ourselves in naked truth, cleansed of the false hope, beliefs and untruths to which we have been clinging. No more strategies, survival mechanisms and holding on. In these moments, we realize there is nothing on which to hang. It's not quite a picnic in the park, but this process of grief can be experienced with less fear and more curiosity. It has the potential to leave us feeling refreshed, renewed, alive and awake. It liberates us from a limiting reality we thought to be our only option.

Each of the feelings, emotions and experiences shared in this book are all part of existing on this planet as a human being. Eventually you will come to have these human experiences in one way or another. For me, understanding that they are part and parcel of being human made me less afraid and less resistant to their presence. Little by little, I chose to step into them, if only lightly, in order to come back into wholeness, remembering all the various parts of myself. Grief is just one of the many portals through which we travel. The analogy of a rocket going into space comes to mind. The boosters are essential to get the rocket into space, but once the rocket is up there, the boosters become unnecessary weight and unless they are relinquished, the space shuttle will never achieve its mission; so, it is with our thoughts and feelings that no longer serve our quest for fulfillment, meaning and satisfaction in our lives.

COACHING QUESTIONS: *What are some boosters in your life that were once essential for bringing you to this moment and that are now obsolete and are holding you back? To what would you say you are committed by holding on to that which no longer serves you? What is left if you choose to let go and make the impossible your path? What will you have to give up in order to make the impossible possible?*

At some point in our lives, almost every one of us loses hope. It's part of our journey and though we look to our religious and spiritual traditions to prepare us for this moment, they cannot. We live in a culture that embraces living and shuns death and unhappy endings. It cannot speak of such things that point to something other than false hope.

Rarely does anyone choose this moment of letting go of hope. Most often, the Universe provides that essential push off the edge of a secure and known world into a chasm of pain, angst and despair. Cancer, accidents, getting fired, retirement, divorce, death of a loved one and war—each of these brings us up against potential endings that spin us out of control; our normal operating procedures malfunction and we collapse into mayhem. Our ideas and beliefs about reality dissolve. Those of you who have had to overcome life crises know of what I speak and most have felt graced by gifts received through the hardship of those circumstances.

To choose deliberately to create the impossible means to create it intentionally in every moment. It is a powerful and courageous choice. Taking the leap out of hope and into the unknown allows you to practice faith, the most powerful virtue of all.

Faith

"Of what use is faith if it is never tested?" Todd Zimmerman

It is easy to practice faith when life is going well. We can feel blessed, lucky and grateful because life is unfolding in a way that feels right, good and effortless. We experience gratitude and thank the gods and goddesses for the blessings bestowed upon us.

Faith is not so easy when things aren't going as planned or when bad things happen or there is no explanation of why things are taking longer to unfold than we planned. Faith is hard to practice when nothing seems to be happening at all. We forget to feel grateful for the gifts being given to us, most often when we no longer see the gifts. When we feel forgotten, powerless and hopeless, the most important thing to practice and the hardest thing to practice is faith.

COACHING QUESTION: *When in your life have you practiced faith? What was the quality of the experience? What does it feel like in your body when you are in faith? Have you found different levels of comfort when practicing faith? How do you exercise and practice faith? How have you learned to rely on it? What is your knowing when it comes to faith?*

Faith is not reasonable, logical and not verifiable. Practicing faith is also not practical. There is no real set of beliefs or structure on which to hold. Even though our religions tell us to live in faith, few actually demonstrate the practice of faith. The strict adherence to dogma, the political cover-ups of religion and spiritualization of religious wars that have harmed and killed millions of people do not reflect a faith-based practice. By living within many religious contexts, we avoid believing in something greater than ourselves to be present for us, especially if it is unseen and unknowable. In order to believe in something greater than ourselves, the ego-self must move out of the driver's seat. It's not that we want to kill the ego; we just want to be at choice. We have been developing a different relationship through this book, maturing our *ego-self* in order to accept a copilot relationship with faith instead of flying single-handed.

In many ways, you practice faith every day naturally and normally. You have faith that you will wake up in the morning; otherwise, you would never go to sleep. You have faith that life will continue and be manageable; otherwise, you would never get out of bed in the morning. You have faith the next generation of children will have the wisdom to heal the wounds of the planet; otherwise, you would not bring new children into this world. This faith is at a less than conscious mind.

Again, it is easy to have faith when things are going well. When they are not going well, it is easy to shift to thinking that something is wrong, unsafe and dangerous and perhaps for some of us, catastrophic. We begin to wonder whether we've done something bad or wrong and we're being punished. "There must be something wrong with me. What did I do to deserve this?" Often, we turn a good god into a wrathful god.

My friend Hector, who is in his mid-sixties, is beginning to think about aging and dying. He is finding himself frustrated, angry and disappointed. He perceives that the world is going to hell in a hand basket. He says he isn't as strong as he was once. For a handyman, this is a frightening moment. His livelihood is at stake. He is *hoping* that he doesn't deteriorate too quickly. He is projecting his powerlessness over his aging process onto *those people* who are screwing up the Earth. He distracts himself from his fears about aging by dating younger women, but he can no longer deny the reality of this human experience of aging. Hope is futile. Resistance is futile. Grief and faith are imminent.

During these opportunities, when faith is one of the few alternatives open to us, we can begin to choose differently. We do this in order to choose to experience our true relationship with ourselves and the Divine in a different way. The following prayer speaks to these moments when we may have no choice, but to surrender to the practice of faith.

"Oh Creator, I am grateful for the way that it is!" Todd Zimmerman

This prayer is one of my favorites. It is short, profound and for me, expresses truth faith. Rather than being grateful only when things are going well, this prayer acknowledges the gifts that are bountiful even when things aren't going so well. In times of despair, when I have said this prayer, a question pops up, "What is there to be grateful for?" This gives me pause to think differently about my circumstances, and I experience the learning and growing that is occurring right now in the midst of my woes. It allows me to see how my thinking and my beliefs limit my capacity to view the world in a bigger way, as a world full of wisdom and love. I'm able, in these moments to have a true knowing that there is Divine presence supporting me every step of the way.

The following prayer is from a twelve-step community. It is simple and comforting in times when faith may seem to be our only companion:

"God, grant me the serenity to accept the things I cannot change, courage to change the things I can and the wisdom to know the difference." The Serenity Prayer

The recovering community has many prayers and affirmations that support individuals in these times when faith is the only handhold. Some affirmations are, "Let go and let God," and "One step at a time."

All of us are in recovery from our addiction to avoiding our true power and purpose. Shifting your relationship to the impossible will put you on your path of recovery that in the end will create endless possibilities.

Faith is not just a religious belief about the God in Heaven that is going to make it okay. I propose that faith is more often born through experience. Without vision of the next handhold or the next foot placement, you learn to trust and hope that you are moving in the right direction. You let go of thinking you should know what to do or where you are going and have faith that you will find your way. As you progress through the many adventures of life, you have the opportunity to gain mastery of surrendering your will when there is nothing else to do, know or *be*. When you get through to the other side and *you will* get to the other side, you will come out with greater wisdom and a greater level of mastery of your life and all the intricate aspects of being human.

Knowing

Those who have faced issues of faith many times, come to a place where trust and faith are not as necessary. They have exercised particular muscles to the degree that there is a level of mastery, confidence and a knowing that Divine wisdom is always and everywhere. They know they are able to handle what needs to be handled. They know by following their bliss, passions, calling and convictions, they will be given what is needed when it is needed. They know they can live in patience and peace while remaining open to allowing what is, to be what it is. Each of us has the capacity to live in this *knowing*, in this peaceful, open and allowing space. We will not get there by living in the safety of the known and the possible while avoiding vulnerability. We will only get there by changing our relationship to the impossible.

Three ways to learn about faith:

Every religion and spiritual tradition has a component of mysticism that is the crucible for faith-based living. Herein lays the heart of faith and true practice of spirituality. There is Christian Mysticism, Judaic Mysticism, Islamic Mysticism and Buddhist Mysticism. My experience is that they can be supportive in your endeavor to live an empowering life in many ways. If you are curious, I would encourage you strongly to research the aspects of your religious and spiritual teachings.

1. Ancient wisdom, passed down for thousands of years is accessible through many indigenous cultures. There are many resources available to research ancient traditions and wisdoms.
2. Acknowledging all of the times you have experienced faith first-hand and survived, perhaps coming out better.

You are being asked to choose consciously a life worth living. If you have read these words then you are at choice about your options. In service to this intention, you might find it empowering to sit with an elder as a mentor or hire a therapist, spiritual director or life coach to support you through this process.

When you live into your true personal power, you face your future and desires without the survival strategies that once distorted your personal truth to avoid vulnerability. Nothing real can be threatened or is in peril. What is threatened is only your attachment to the beliefs and interpretations by which you have lived. Experiment by letting go just a little bit and begin to create the impossible!

Practice Areas

- Go through your life history and write down all the events that you witnessed, heard or had happen to you that seemed impossible. For example—I contracted polio when I was two years old. Everyone was certain I would die. The doctors sent my parents home with a dying child. I didn't die and I do not have any of the handicaps found in most polio victims. Impossible! I believe we all have dozens of events to report. I'm going to ask you not to censor your stories. Don't assess the level of impossibility. What windfalls, what weird and wacky or spiritual events happened that seemed impossible, but happened to you or to people you know?
- Journal your thoughts and feelings for each of the impossibilities you listed. How did you make sense of that event and your part in it? What did you decide about you, about the world, about impossibility? I have a belief that good things only happen to other people and never to me. That's something I decided when I saw other people get the big prize, win the lottery, are chosen for the lead roles.
- As you journal, recognize patters of thinking that are true and those that are not necessarily true, but you choose to *believe* them to be true. List these beliefs.
- Notice which of these beliefs actually *serve you* in moving toward that which you say you want and which ones *hold you* hostage to a life that is less than fulfilling.
- As you distinguish these thoughts and beliefs, notice how you are *being* with them. This is the *be with* process. There is nothing to fix or heal through doing. In this moment, it's a matter of noticing how you *be* with this. Are you being frustrated, helpless, anxious, worried or guilty? Just notice your emotional state and then notice how you feel about being in these states. "I'm angry that I am being powerless to change what isn't working for me. I'm sad that I am being unconfident to accept that I have what it takes to…"
- See if you can shift this feeling about how you are feeling to something closer to acceptance. Practice saying to yourself, "I accept that in this present moment, I feel helpless, angry or frustrated."

- What, if anything shifted by accepting yourself in this present moment? Write it down.
    - What becomes possible by accepting your present condition?

Chapter 5: Accountability and Responsibility

One of the most self-empowering things you can do for yourself is to begin taking responsibility for how your life is turning out and then be accountable for your words and for your actions. Without responsibility and accountability, it is very unlikely that you will create the life you want. I guarantee it!

The intention of this chapter is to distinguish accountability from responsibility by investigating when and how you are being accountable for agreements you make and for the circumstances in your life. We will also look at the concept of integrity and what it means in relation to everything discussed this far in the book.

COACHING QUESTIONS: *Think back to when you were a child. List the responsibilities given to you and with which you had no choice, but to comply, as opposed to the agreements you entered into freely and consciously. See if you can feel the physical sensations of the times when it didn't feel right or felt out of alignment with your truth to comply. What attitudes, beliefs and/or interpretations were created in order to support you through those responsibilities? How were you held accountable by others and how did you hold yourself accountable?*

As an adult, how are you still influenced by your earlier choices and decision regarding responsibility and accountability? How effective is this way of thinking and being in relation to what you say you want now? How is it working for you? Are there different ways of thinking that will support a more effective relationship with responsibility and accountability?

I received an email this morning from an upcoming student. She was requesting some clarification on a starting date of a program I promised about six weeks ago. My response was, I promised again to get back to her today with a date and time for the program. What is my responsibility? To whom am I responsible? What is accountability in relation to my responsibility? To what and whom am I accountable?

What's the Difference

I've struggled for years to understand the relationship between responsibility and accountability. I have persevered because I think it is an important distinction. Here's what I've come up with:

Responsibility

Responsibility is the obligation to carry forward an assigned or agreed upon task to a successful conclusion. It is yours to do through explicit agreement or because there is an edict or law. With responsibility comes self-empowerment and self-authority to direct and take necessary action to ensure success.

I have a responsibility to my students to provide materials and courses to support the intended goals and outcomes. I am responsible for my agreement to follow through with my word and my promise. As a graduate, I am responsible to those who taught me and I am responsible for providing a program in alignment with the Institutions high standards of education. I am responsible to myself because I have a level of integrity that I must meet in order to be in alignment and in right-relationship with myself. I am responsible because I knowingly entered into an agreement with the school, students and myself to provide the most effective course and training program in transformational coaching.

There are aspects of our lives for which we are responsible because there are rules and laws to which must be adhered. I am responsible to the laws that protect others and me from harm. I drive the speed limits (most of the time anyway), I stop at stop signs and stoplights. My work complies with the code of ethics for coaches and therapists and I show up on time to my coaching sessions and my classes. These things are expected of me and I am responsible for adhering to these codes of conduct.

Accountability

A person is accountable to follow through with the task agreed upon, the action or conduct for which you agreed to be responsible. One has a responsibility to oneself and to others. Accountability is the process of fulfilling the agreement. Responsibility doesn't shift until there is a completion of the agreement and neither does accountability. Responsibility is the agreement phase of a relationship and accountability is the action phase.

With accountability, there is an obligation to inform yourself or another person about your completion of the task or action upon which you agreed. Though it sounds absurd to inform yourself about something, from a coach's perspective, there is an essential requirement in becoming an adult to hold yourself accountable for your actions and your words. Unfortunately, we don't see this level of accountability very often. I believe all of us suffer from the consequences or lack of accountability. I believe business and marriage partnerships would run smoother and parenting would be far more effortless for mom and dad and easier on the children.

Learning the Difference Between Responsibility and Accountability

As children, we were responsible for living within specific agreements regarding home, life, education and religion. We had to be accountable to our parents for doing the dishes, cleaning our room or feeding the dog. We were accountable to our teachers for getting our homework done on time. We were accountable to coaches, priests, ministers and all kinds of people who held us accountable for action and inaction towards the agreements we made.

As adults, we have a responsibility to care for others and ourselves in a mature and respectful way. Each of us has a unique style of being responsible that comes with the authority to direct and take the necessary actions to ensure success. As adults, to whom are we accountable for ensuring success?

Depending on how we set up our life and work agreements—our responsibilities—we are accountable to bosses, spouses, community, the law, ministers and just about everyone. Underlying all of these relationships is the relationship we have with ourselves. Being in right-relationship with self, means being *responsible* to our values and the agreements we've made to ourselves about our dreams and visions. It means being accountable to ourselves first; however, I go out on a limb to say, most of do not hold ourselves accountable enough. *Enough? What* is *enough? Enough* is the degree to which you say what you mean and mean what you say. You take the actions in alignment with a commitment in order to achieve the outcome you want. *Enough* can get you by, but it may be less self-empowering and feel less than great. You know what it feels like when you are being accountable *enough.* There is a quality of being accountable that feels honest, free, productive, creative, fun and satisfying. The quality of not being accountable feels sticky, irritating and uncomfortable. It makes me want to do something in order not to feel these feelings.

Do you ever wonder why there are so many twelve-step programs in the world? They are terrific mechanisms for accountability. With joining a twelve-step program comes the opportunity to participate with a community of like-minded individuals who have learned, as most of has have, how to absolve ourselves of accountability for our responsibilities. Through denial, excuses, justifications and rationalizations, we slide out of right-relationship with others and with ourselves. Whatever drug of choice we use—chemicals, alcohol, sex, love, guilt, worry, eating and victimization of others and ourselves, we are using a survival strategy that absolves us or relieves us of the anxiety of being ineffective toward any responsibility or accountability. The twelve-step organizations give us a place and a community to support right-relationship with ourselves and with others by providing time, space and a container within which an individual can demonstrate personal accountability.

Why So Little Accountability

COACHING QUESTIONS: *To what degree would you say you are accountable for your thoughts, actions and your life? How did you come to decide to be accountable to this degree? What works by being accountable at this level? What doesn't work? How do you rationalize and justify coming up short on your agreements to yourself and to others? Make a list of things you say to get you off the hook.*

If I admit to you that I don't follow through with my agreements, you would think I am irresponsible, careless and negligent. To some degree, you would be right. If you were my boss, you probably wouldn't promote me or you might fire me, which makes perfect sense because I am not showing up to do my responsibilities. If you were my partner or spouse, you might think less of me and over time, you had decided to leave me. If you were my students, you might ignore what I am teaching you. If I don't disclose my lack of accountability, I'm hoping you won't find out and decide that I am lax and irresponsible. I pretend you don't see my lack of accountability and you pretend it doesn't bother you, until it does.

Punitive actions on the part of parents and siblings, nuns and teachers, certainly kept me from telling the truth. Constant threats of rejection, abandonment, embarrassment, shame and blame; you know what I am talking about. Very few of us grow up deciding that it's better to tell the truth than to lie. We are told that it is better to tell the truth, but we all know it's not. Religions, political systems, educational institutions and judicial systems all talk about the value and importance of truth, but each of these systems exhibit the game of who can lie the best, not who is being accountable for their truths. There is a double standard in which we try to live. How are you *being* with the lack of accountability and integrity that shows up in so many life–impacting situations? If you are not accountable in a world that isn't accountable, you can ride the wave. "I will pretend I don't see your lack of integrity and you pretend you don't see mine." All of us compromise ourselves, fearful of the repercussions of being found out. It's an epidemic in every aspect of our culture and our lives.

Case in Point: The Use of False Humility to Avoid Right-Relationship with Self

Here is an example to demonstrate a lack of accountability with self by using false humility and appeasing *tribal chords* strategically. The outcome is profound.

My client Magi is brilliant, loving, kind and very generous. She is one of the rare individuals who at the age of 45 has the passion and enthusiasm of a young child. Magi and I began our work together because of her interest in becoming a coach. Through the development of her practice and over the course of the months we worked together, our conversation changed its focus from what actions she needed to take to what actions she needed to stop.

Over time, it became clear that Magi has been giving herself away. She gives away her time, gifts, talents and professional knowledge and work. When we began to explore this, she revealed a degree of shame she felt for being gifted and talented. This showed up as false humility. It showed up as not allowing the full expression of her brilliance. It was like putting a bushel basket over her head so she didn't shine so brightly, but it was Magi herself who put the basket over her head.

"You should be more generous to your brother." Magi's father would say. "You need to give to others who have less than you, and you should always give them the *best* and take what's left for yourself." This is what Magi heard. What became clear as a child was that it wasn't all right to be gifted and talented. Magi decided that she was not okay as she was. In order to be accepted, feel less shame and less guilt, she would have to minimize her brilliance so she wouldn't outshine her brother, other family members, friends or anyone who seemed less gifted.

To feel okay, Magi learned to give herself away. She learned to minimize a compliment and diminish the contrast between herself and her siblings. She dumbed herself down to stay less obvious and be more appropriate in her small town. She learned to feel responsible to those less fortunate than herself. "I should take care of others because I have the gifts and ability to do so."

When she left home to start a new life, Magi felt guilty for leaving her family and community behind, but in many ways, she never really left. Though she has created an amazing life for herself, Magi still carries the guilt of being more than, better than or greater than. Her work is to individuate; to distinguish herself from the disempowering thoughts she carried about herself for decades.

Magi is out of integrity with herself in a number of ways.

1. She isn't in right-relationship with herself in that she hasn't allowed herself to own her brilliance and delight.

2. She created a sense of responsibility for her family as a strategy to avoid feeling shame for having gifts and talents. It eases the guilt when she is overly generous with what is hers. "I should give it away. I have it and they don't" This is a form of enabling. Her family doesn't get to grow themselves because Magi's guilt kept her in servitude to their emotional wounds. They need to take care of their own emotional wounds and she needs to take care of hers.

3. False humility as a strategy keeps Magi from living her life in a bigger way. She gets to play small, diminishing her power in support of eliminating the possibility for envy, jealousy and resentment. She is a very nice person in order to ensure she is lovable and likable.

4. Magi is being self-deprecating. As she struggles with her true nature as a brilliant and lovable woman, she is developing a different language and a different way of being. This new way of being allows her to take off the bushel basket and acknowledge humility that rides sidekick to her brilliance. This is an important conversation we'll tackle shortly.

This is a very subtle conversation in relation to accountability and responsibility, but it is crucial that it be recognized for the power it has to cripple the most talented and brilliant minds on the planet. I mean *every child born.*

Whether you have brilliance and many talents or whether you have few, each of you made a decision about how to *be* with what you got. Each story shared in this book is about an individual who, as a child, decided to some degree that he or she lacked worth, value and lovability. Their journey to themselves and to that which they say they want continues to reveal new levels of conversations that have held them hostage. The mental gymnastics that we go through to navigate the obstacle course of everyday life takes an enormous toll on our bodies and our emotions. We try to please everyone—everyone as we think them to be, because so many of us are hiding behind our façade, masking our truth for fear we will be found out for our greatnesses or our foibles. It's hard to know who they really are.

Depression Due to Lack of Accountability

One of the most useful explanations for depression I have ever come across is that it's caused most often by self-deprecating thoughts, speech and action. When I express myself in self-deprecating behavior, it instills in me a sense of powerlessness and helplessness. It generates feelings of guilt and shame. Inevitably, I want to numb out and find ways to feel good.

All of us employ some form of self-deprecation. Any time we rationalize, justify and make excuses for our actions, we are being self-deprecating. At the same time, we are avoiding accountability and responsibility for our actions; we are not honoring our truth. Any time we diminish our well-being for the sake of another, we are being *self-deprecating.* We are not honoring what we require for a fulfilling and nourished life. When we discount our wants and needs or apologize without cause, we are being self-deprecating and avoiding confrontation, most likely by diminishing our truth. When we reduce scheduled playtime for work, we are being self-deprecating by minimizing requirements for a balanced life. Avoiding speaking our truth is self-deprecating. Any time we self-deprecate, we are to some degree, not being in integrity or accountable and invariably creating depression. **Depression**, in the truest sense of the word, is the numbing out of feelings and sensations that direct us toward right-relationship with self, in service to safety, security and avoiding the risk of rejection, shame and abandonment. Numbing out is the process whereby we anesthetize ourselves from feeling anything and everything.

I find it very valuable to listen for how each of my clients self-deprecates. How does this client put herself down, putting herself second, diminishing her value, worth and truth? Magi is a great example of a high-functioning individual, but still self-deprecates with the consequence being that she could anesthetize herself from feeling the shame and guilt of being brilliant. Christina is another good example of someone who was doing everything she could to avoid accountability and responsibility in her life through self-deprecating thoughts, speech and action, with the outcome of depression. She too has limited her power to generate a great life by staying within the confines of n*ot too smart*.

Christina

Christina is 43 years old and suffers from obesity and diabetes. During the past three years, she has been in a working partnership with Lois, who is abusive verbally to Christina. She berates Christina constantly. Until just recently, Christina has been taking full responsibility for all her problems, including being abused by Lois. Christina indicated that she isn't capable of taking care of herself or her diabetes. "If I would only work harder, Lois wouldn't yell at me and would stop calling me a loser. If I were more disciplined with exercise and diet, I wouldn't have caused the diabetes. If I weren't such a slob in the first place, I could clean up my act and have a life worth living." This is what taking responsibility looks like to an individual who uses self-deprecating thoughts and actions as a survival strategy to avoid a more authentic form of responsibility and accountability; a form that requires confronting conversations with others and herself. What is left is depression, a quality of being that carries with it hopelessness, powerlessness, ineptness, shame and guilt. The more depressed Christina feels, the more likely she is to hold her depression responsible for her life and her circumstances. She has come to believe that she cannot find whatever it is she needs to feel better in her life because she's depressed. To whom is Christina accountable when an emotional state, such as depression is the perceived perpetrator of her hopelessness and powerlessness?

Christina requested coaching because she wanted an exit strategy from her partnership with Lois. She also wanted to take care of her body to diminish the diabetic symptoms from which she suffered. What lies underneath is her self-deprecating strategies and the depression that ensues. My coaching agreement with Christina was to support her in taking care of her health and her partnership with Lois. My experience as a therapist and a coach has been that the depression would dissolve once Christina began utilizing self-empowering strategies in her life daily.

"I am responsible for how my life is turning out. I'm wrong and a failure because I make bad choices and I don't trust myself to make good choices." Christina sobs out her life-long woes of being depressed, out of control, continually bringing chaos into her life and living with diabetes in a way that doesn't support her health or well-being. She says she is ready to change and ready to feel better. Her comment about being responsible for how her life is turning out indicates a failure on her part to do it *right*.

Over the following months, Christina began to get a clearer picture, one that reflected an old paradigm. The choices she had made came from accountability in the service of safety and avoiding risk. Her childhood was full of abuse, betrayal and rejection. By playing the role of a passive and helpless victim she came to believe that *is who she is.* Initially, Christina was so sure that she could not trust herself that she almost had me convinced. If she succeeded in convincing me, I would not have been an effective coach. I would have been caught in the web of her illusion of powerlessness and I would have colluded with her. I put a proverbial stake in the ground and tied us both to it with the belief that if she is creative enough to manufacture all of this drama, then she is certainly creative enough to generate a diversity of alternatives that will give her a life full of health, peace, love and playfulness.

From a place of hopeless and helpless victim (Christina is a victim of being self-deprecating) she doesn't have a chance, but through the practice of noticing how she deploys particular strategies in order to avoid true accountability for her life, those that are in alignment with her highest truth and highest good, Christina has been able to see how she intentionally self-deprecates and how she creates the experience of being depressed.

Through self-observation, Christina began to see things differently. Rather than seeing herself as the cause of Lois's abuse; therefore, shaming and blaming herself, she was able give back to Lois the responsibility for her emotional outbursts. Christina was then free to recognize and be responsible for her reactions and responses to Lois and the abuse. If she can see how she created these dynamics intentionally, then perhaps she can see that she is not so disabled and helpless as she thought once.

One aspect of Christina wanted to make her responsible for the abuse from Lois. This made her feel as though she had some power in the situation; however, another part of Christina wanted to make Lois responsible. She wanted to make all of her issues (i.e. diabetes, sexual abuse, betrayal and abandonment by her father, siblings and ex-husband and her obesity), responsible for her unhappiness. When she convinced herself that her circumstances had nothing to do with her, she didn't have to be accountable and could continue to be out of control, powerless and helpless. She wanted to make the problems about being victimized by life and circumstances, about being wounded and damaged; therefore, incapable of creating change on her own.

How does someone gain accountability after decades of believing the world is responsible for her circumstances? Through practice!

Last Friday, Christina confronted Lois through an email. It was an act of self-empowering accountability for her responsibility to her own truth, well-being and her brilliant work. She articulated clearly that she wasn't willing to work under the present circumstances with Lois and rather than continue to be bullied and threatened, she quit! The degree of clarity, presence and honoring of herself in this letter between her and Lois was astonishing. This was not the same woman I met five months ago. She had transformed herself by being accountable for her emotions, thoughts, beliefs and attitudes. She became accountable to her truth. She followed through on her convictions. She discovered within herself a way to swim out from beneath the burdensome experiences that held her under; her beliefs that she was a depressed and wimpy loser.

Entrenched as she was in her story, Christina is trusting that she can make a difference in her own life. This woman creates a software product that interfaces with other software products. In my mind, she is a creative genius in her ability to both conceptualize and manifest reality in the context of her work. If she can do this, then she can conceptualize a new way of being in her life and manifest that too. The only difference is the degree to which she is committed to having the life she says she wants. She is demonstrating responsibility for her well-being by taking action to leave her partnership. She is taking more pride in her ability to follow through with her intentions, being more accountable to her clients, to me as her coach and most importantly, she is being more accountable to herself. She is able to allow herself to be witnessed through our sessions and is learning the value and importance of integrity.

How do We Let Ourselves Off the Hook

Like Christina, we all want to make someone or something outside ourselves responsible for our problems. That's the way we avoid agreements, accountability and ourselves. We avoid getting to know who we are and how we are *being out of control* in our lives. Not out of control as in a psychotic break or a nervous breakdown, but out of control as in relinquishing control, giving it to other people for the sake of maintaining a sense of security and safety. More importantly, we give our power to some aspect of ourselves that would rather suffer, settle and survive. This aspect isn't interested in changing because it doesn't want to lose the security of what it has and what it knows.

We all know the aspects of ourselves that have different wants and needs. Part of me wants to lose ten pounds and I want to be accountable to that. Another part of me wants to eat whatever I want, whenever I want. I need to be accountable to that too. If I lose weight, am I being accountable? If I gain weight, am I being accountable? Which part gets what it wants? I just step on the scale, look at the little arrow and I can see who's winning the battle. Yes, we are in relationships with others who confront us in any number of ways. Many of us have been abused physically, sexually and emotionally. The memories of these experiences bring up feelings and sensations that we want to suppress and forget. If these memories and experiences are getting in the way of you being self-empowered, I encourage you strongly to enlist support from a therapist or coach who can empower you to work through these issues. This will free you to navigate the course of your life more effectively and with much less effort. The conversations each of us has with our self can either interfere with or support empowered speaking of our truth.

Avoiding Vulnerability

Over the past few weeks as I write this chapter, I had several opportunities to get clear about where I'm not being accountable to others and myself. I say I want to write, but how much time do I really spend writing? I say I'm affected by the way a friend of mine is being, but I'm not speaking to her about it. I've realized that during my first marriage, my behaviors were hurtful to my ex-husband, but I've not shared that realization with him. I have students who are pushing my buttons and I have been letting them get away with it. I promised myself more playtime, but when I check my emails, I get absorbed and all my playtime is used up. Am I being accountable?

As a coach, trainer and facilitator of transformation, not only do I want to look as if I'm working my own program, I actually want to work the program! I feel fantastic when I am being authentic, creative, productive and playful; however, at the same time, I hate working my own program. It challenges every fiber of my being. I'm open to attacks and ridicule from others, but most of all from myself. I'm vulnerable and exposed. I'm angry that I have to be open, vulnerable and exposed. I'm scared that, despite all of the work I have done to get here, wherever *here* is, it is still going to be ugly, hurtful and frankly, I don't want to deal with the fallout. Even though I'm fearful of the ugly and hurtful fallout, evidence shows that I'm far more confident, comfortable and capable to handle confrontation that comes about.

Obviously, I'm not being forced to be clear, truthful, authentic and accountable; it's a personal choice. Based on the principles I espouse and mostly live by, I want to stay in my integrity. My experience is, when I am not in integrity and aligned with my highest truth, as I know it in this present moment, somehow and somewhere, inevitably I will be put on the proverbial rack. I either stretch my comfort zone and allow responses that the coward-self in me wants to avoid or I continue with my normal operating procedures, knowing that the ties that bind me to the rack will only create more tension and stress, disabling me in one form or another. AAAAAHHHHH! AAHHHHH!

Integrity

COACHING QUESTIONS: *What is integrity to you? What is the quality of the experience when you are* being in *integrity? What is the quality of the experience of* being out *of integrity? To what degree do you live with this experience or sensation in your body what would you need to shift in order to be more in integrity? Of what would you have to let go? What is missing that if it were present would allow more integrity?*

Integrity is living in alignment with your beliefs and your word. If your words and your actions are not inline, you are being out of integrity. Integrity is being accountable to your word. Your word is the only thing you have that supports relationship with others and with yourself. Your word comes across not only verbally, but also through the way, you are *being*. So, how are you being with yourself and with others?

Without integrity, your word has no meaning or value. It is just gibberish and noise to fill up space. You break promises to yourself and others. People cannot trust you and you cannot trust you. Self-empowerment is a joke without integrity.

We *prostitute* our energy, words, ideas and intentions in the name of safety and security. My desire is for each of us to begin considering the possibility of a different way of being; a way of being that allows compassion for oneself while in this adventure and investigation of discovering, revealing and unconcealing our individual truths and then being accountable to them.

It is not an easy process to take responsibility for your life and then be accountable for how you are showing up in it. It can be extremely intriguing and rewarding when filled with curiosity and fascination especially if you remove the judgments of right, wrong, good and bad. By suspending judgments, you can look at your life and your relationships based on what you decided to believe when you were younger. At that time, you didn't have the wisdom and maturity you have today. Today you have the capacity to see things differently, assess things differently and choose differently, only because you say so!

Practice Areas

- Notice when and where you express yourself as a victim.
- Notice when you take responsibility for other people's problems, pain and suffering.
- Notice when you avoid taking responsibility for the suffering you cause others and yourself.
- Create opportunities to acknowledge yourself for things you do well, for your brilliance and creativity and for kindness to others and yourself.
- Acknowledge when you have accomplished what you have set out to do. Celebrate your accomplishments!
- Notice body sensations that communicate that you are being in integrity.
- Notice body sensations that communicate that you are not being in integrity.

- Begin to practice acknowledging yourself when you are and when you are not being in integrity. Use a coach, friend, therapist or a mentor for support.
- Begin to speak the truth to others when you are not being accountable to the agreements you have made with them.
- Consider doing a "Fourth Step" from a twelve-step program. Make a list, a moral inventory of all harms committed against others and yourself.
- See yourself not as someone who has failed to live up to your agreements, but as someone who has maintained allegiances to values that conflict with truth, integrity and accountability.
- Look for signs of compassion in yourself and for yourself.
- Don't try to forgive yourself and don't try to get forgiveness from others. When you allow yourself disclosure of the truths of how you came to be *the* you that reads this book, there will be no need for lying and forgiveness will come effortlessly.

Chapter 6: Commitments

Intention, Conviction, Commitment and Discipline

"You've got to have a dream; if you don't have a dream, how you gonna have a dream come true?" Rogers and Hammerstein, *South Pacific*

What is it that turns a wish, dream or desire into fulfillment? Much of the self-help literature suggests that you have to know what you want first, being clear about the degree to which you are intentional about manifesting that desire is second, third is, you have to embody the experience of having what you desire already and last, you let go of your attachment to the wanting.

We have discussed some of these steps in previous chapters. The focus of this chapter is self-empowerment through setting your intentions, engaging confidence and conviction, committing and then with discipline, following through with the necessary actions to have what you say you want.

COACHING QUESTIONS: *What were some of your intentions when you bought this book? What did you want? What did you hope to gain? How have you been* being *with the coaching questions and practice areas? To what degree have you been committed to having what you say you want from this book? What conflicting commitments have been present that may have you avoid answering the coaching questions or doing the practice areas? To what degree have you disciplined yourself to ensure the outcome you desired by reading this book? What is at risk if you were to have what you say you want? What would have to change for you to have what you say you want?*

The Road to Hell is Paved with Good Intentions

Many of us who read self-help books usually do not do the exercises that will actualize the desired results we seek. In fact, most of us don't follow through with many intentions we set for ourselves. This is not to shame or point a finger at anyone; it's just a fact. I would say I want what I want, and I want it in a form that transforms me magically into *the me* that gets everything I desire;

therefore, I read self-help books with the *hope* that just the process of reading it will do the trick. It won't. The reason it won't is because I am not willing enough to take action in accordance with what I say I want. My level of conviction doesn't support me to think or act differently inside my skin. I'm not committed enough to exercise and discipline the muscles it takes to create that which I say I want.

During challenging times in my life, I was suffering enough that I followed through with the suggested practices and exercises found within particular books. My intentions were strong enough to push through my desire to avoid risk and vulnerability. Self-empowerment was imbedded in the process of alleviating the suffering, but it wasn't my primary focus or intention. I just wanted the pain to go away. Over time though, as I followed through with the exercises and practices, the pain did go away and a different measure of self-empowerment became apparent.

COACHING QUESTIONS: *What is the quality of the experience of* wanting *or* having intentions*? Intensify that experience. What is it like now? Intensify it more and see what that's like.*

"I'm now just letting myself want and at the same time, I get mad at myself for wanting. I used to deny that I wanted anything. I like having. I like having what I want. I get what I want and I like that, but I don't like the feeling of vulnerability that comes with wanting." Stephanie

The experience of wanting can be very uncomfortable for people. They experience anxiety, nervousness and vulnerability. For others, there is excitement, anticipation and expectancy. What creates these different responses? The vulnerability of wanting is embedded in our bodies, as are the memories of disappointment. The level of significance we give to what we want influences our willingness to have a want, enough to set intentions to make it happen. More people than you can imagine have given up wanting, not because it's part of their spiritual practice, but because they decided long ago that it wasn't safe to want, and most likely they weren't going to get it, so they stopped wanting.

Buddhist traditions say that wanting creates suffering. As a spiritual concept, this in itself creates suffering. We can't *not* want. Wanting drives our movements toward the future. It drives us to take baths, be healthy, procreate, love, learn and create. What creates the suffering is our attachment to our wanting. We suffer when our wants are not satisfied in specific ways. The wanting in itself is just an experience. We add the attachment, meaning and/or significance to it. This is what brings about the suffering.

The practice of having a want, setting the intention to create the actions and follow-through to support the intentions, while at the same time, not being attached to the wanting or the outcome, is essential. Living in the moment and practicing these steps strengthens character and gives us the courage to live into the unknown and the wisdom and confidence to be with whatever shows up.

Each of us has a particular level of conviction, beyond commitment and beyond discipline, for life to turn out the way we say we want. Either it is enough to take us over the edge of our hopes, fears and failures, into the life we imagine or it's not. My work as a Transformational Coach is to support individuals and organizations in living into their fullest potential, out beyond the edge of their comfort zone and into the impossible. The only way to do this is by investigating this territory. We have to take the leap.

Desire without Commitment and/or Conviction

This isn't one of those stories that end with the client living into the impossible, not at this time anyway. This story is about the commitment to stay safe and invulnerable.

Frances is more committed to security, stability and invulnerability than she is to manifesting the life she says she wants. Rather than face her interpretations and beliefs that hold her back, she is choosing to employ another teacher, another coach and trainer to give her the skills and tools she is afraid she lacks. She is doing this to maintain the income she has been making in the corporate world while creating a life and career. This life and career shifts and mutates quite often for her. There are always hopes and dreams, but until there is conviction, she will be unhappy in her security and confused about what she should do next. She will be wondering anxiously why life isn't giving her what she says she wants.

Frances has worked in Corporate America for 12 years and in many capacities. She earns an average of $175,000 per year. In two months, she will be let go from her position with a very nice stipend, a package that will carry her through the next twelve months without having to work.

Frances and I have worked together for a couple of years on various projects. She calls me when she is feeling very heartfelt about a particular desire she wants to achieve and after a few weeks, her interests wane and she disappears from coaching only to return a few months down the road with a new passion.

Four weeks ago, this talented, brilliant, but skittish woman called me expressing a deep passion and longing to write and wanted to set up some time to work together toward creating a writing career. She and I had talked about a writing career many times, but on this particular day, her request for coaching felt different. She sounded very committed. During this time, she was also facing the possibility of changing her job or losing it altogether and that is what happened in the end. She had been working with a career counselor and a psychic to support her through this transition. She was becoming clearer that she wanted to bring writing in as part of her life's vocation, along with a variety of work she would have to take on in order to support herself. Frances wanted to continue making no less than $150,000 per year. Her desire was to continue to work in an environment in which she could make that kind of money and still have the time and energy to create a writing practice. Frances was ready to create the impossible.

Having gone a number of rounds with Frances, I knew her to use particular strategies. The one I expected to surface in our work together allows a particular desire to be expressed and commitment made. Then, she is caught in some tangent that inevitably leads to a dead end. She disappears from our coaching at this point to follow another coach, teacher or guru. This time; however, I set some parameters that would allow us some consistency over time and a deeper level of clarity. We agreed that, instead of our usual every-other-week sessions, we would meet weekly until the momentum of her writing was carrying her consistently over any obstacles in her way. I was explicit that at a time when she would want to leave coaching before achieving her goals, I would reflect back to her very clearly her strategies to avoid manifesting her dreams. It didn't take long for her strategies to come out to play.

More than anything, Frances is committed to security, stability and avoidance of risk. From our first session almost two years ago, the underlying tenor has been to maintain her safety net, no matter what. She has wanted a relationship with a man for love, but more importantly, for security. Many times, she has talked of leaving her job in order to create a retreat center where corporate leaders could come and advance themselves. Innovation inspires Frances and she wanted to bring this to the world in a wonderful way; perhaps a retreat center in somewhere in Ireland that was accessible to many international leaders and innovators. The dilemma was that Frances would have to risk the security of her current situation, her current stability in the corporate world for her dreams. She wanted to incorporate her writing, public speaking, corporate background and coaching into a remarkable environment, but she would have to take a leap of faith off the edge of her comfort zone.

We created a list together of what needed to be thought about, just the visualizing and imagination stage of things, the thinking part of the task. Not long after this session, Frances was back in the pool of her conversation, fearing the risk and loss of security and stability.

Frances takes advantage of the many workshops and retreats that are available in the San Francisco Area where she lives. She's found many people that she believes can guide her and provide the tools that will support her in living her life purpose. She's looking for someone who will take her under their wing, teach and guide her and inevitably take care of her while she gets her practice up and running. Her underlying belief is that she can't succeed on her own. She needs someone or something to ensure her financial safety and security. This belief holds her hostage, binding her to fears transmitted to her long ago by her mother. It doesn't matter where beliefs originate, only that we empower them to undo us and undo our commitment to generate the outcome we desire.

One more thing about Frances; she has been told that she is an intuitive healer and has many gifts that will support others. I have no doubt that this is true and this is what Frances says she wants, more than anything; however, that dog-gone security thing keeps showing up any time she takes steps toward her desires. I was hoping that we could confront her fears and that her level of conviction was strong enough to get her through this process.

Just two weeks, after our latest agreement to meet on a weekly basis, Frances called to postpone our session. It had to do with a conflicting meeting at work. This time, we were able to reschedule within the week. The following week, the same thing happened, except this time we had to postpone for almost two weeks. Yesterday, Frances called to cancel our sessions altogether. She said she has been doing some deep inner work and needed some time to process it on her own. I was dreading this conversation, but had anticipated it ever since our recommitment to work together just a few weeks earlier.

I inquired about her reason for having to process this alone, why not with a coach. She held a number of illegitimate excuses. I reiterated our agreement about our weekly sessions and about this very moment when we would talk about her survival strategies and how they would have her disappear once again from coaching. The big *yes, but* surfaced. "Yes, but our agreement was to get me to write and this isn't about that. This is about my future and what I am going to do with it." She retorted. France's *yes, buts* have been buying her lots of freedom in her life, but they are full of rationalizations and justifications for not following through with her commitment. She was back-pedaling out of her commitment, slipping and sliding away. We talked for perhaps 10 minutes altogether. I shared with her my observations of her strategies and she acknowledged the truth of them; however, she felt she really needed this time to herself.

The Fierceness of Commitment and/or Conviction

I often ask my clients to assess their level of commitment to their desired goal. The question goes something like this; "On a scale from one to 100, to what degree are you truly in alignment with your goal to create what you say you want successfully and powerfully? Which aspects of you are more aligned with maintaining the status quo, stability, security and avoiding risk?" Through this line of inquiry, they are able to see that maybe they aren't 100% in line with their dreams and that there is other things to which they are more committed. It's great to get this all distinguished so they can gauge where they are in relation to their values, intentions, and responsibilities.

You can spend your whole life wishing and hoping and never leave the comforts of your easy chair. Millions of armchair sailors dream of that adventurous passage to some exotic destination, but the majority of boat owners will never get their boats out of the harbor. It's enough for most of them to face their day-to-day destinations.

It takes a great deal of courage to look every day in the face with the hope of it being better than yesterday. Very few of us are actually committed enough to make damn sure it is an exceptional day, every day. A fierce conviction is required of those who are invested in having a great life and empowering themselves to live their lives this way. The challenge is to continue to clear our thinking mind and our emotional bodies of the stuff that wants to return to the safe ground of, "It's impossible. I can't do this."

The Qualities of Conviction: You Don't Know Them Until You Feel Them

Our somatic or physical reaction to the world is the *tell-all* of our reality. If you want to know what's true for you, go to the source—your body—it never lies. Do you want to know if your convictions are strong? Check inside and feel it. How do you know if what you are feeling is a conviction or something else? What is the quality of conviction?

Put down the book and close your eyes. With your eyes closed, lower your vision, as though you were looking at your lap. For a few moments, just feel the sensations in your body; scan for particular feelings or a felt-sense of yourself. Now, bring in the world *conviction* and think about something for which you have strong conviction. It can be peace, love, or maybe the well-being of your children. What feelings or sensations appear? Stay with the exploration. Give yourself the freedom to investigate deeply the qualities of being that are connected to this concept. Take some time to write down your findings.

When I practice this exercise, I get a felt-sense of a strong hold in my chest, not a clenching, but a strong and fierce presence; my chest pushes out, making more room for my heart. The word *courage* comes to mind. The word *courage* in French means, *open heart.* My chest expands to make room for courage.

In my abdomen, I have a felt-sense of power, a kind of a protecting armor that allows me to do battle with what is coming my way that may try to stop or impede me from my mission.

In my throat, I feel a clarity of knowing what is mine to do. I may not know the specific actions I will be taking, but I know that I will know when the time is right.

I also have an experience of sadness or grief. My felt-sense of conviction in this moment is so strong that I'm willing to let go of everything I know and have, in order to move into whatever it takes. I begin to feel my sadness. It's daunting to live into something when you don't know the outcome.

In my head, I have the felt-sense of determination, resolve, willpower and fortitude.

If you can feel these qualities of conviction either through witnessing others or through your own desires to *win*, then you know that you have been here, to a place that has been a driving force in your life, relationships and your desire to fulfill a dream or to do the impossible. How? Why? Because you say so!

Many comic book heroes (e.g. Spiderman, Superman, Wonder Woman, etc.) display conviction and commitment in high definition, fervor, vehemence and passion. Their mission is to protect the innocent and the good against evil and injustice. We don't question Spidey's level of commitment or conviction, we know he's gonna come through for us.

You've seen movies that portray a father or mother who is dead-set on rescuing their child from danger and life-threatening situations. Denzel Washington portrayed a parent in the movie, *John Q,* where there was no doubt that his conviction to save his son's life was for real. In the movie, he took the entire emergency ward hostage until they decided to give his son a heart transplant that would save his son's life. He showed us what it was like.

Television shows such as *Survivor, American Idol* and *Dancing with the Stars* are great to watch because they give us an opportunity to witness what doing the impossible looks like in ordinary people. We watch people work relentlessly to achieve their goals. We see what it looks like when people fail, give up and lose.

COACHING QUESTIONS: *What are some things, projects or relationships about which you have strong convictions? List them in the order of the strength of conviction you feel. Which of these projects or relationships are you working on consciously, with intention and conviction? Which ones are not getting the attention you would like them to get? What is getting in the way? How are you avoiding or distracting yourself from completing these projects? Of what are you afraid you would have to give up or let go if you brought these projects or relationships to their full potential or completion? What is missing that, if it were present, would allow you to do that?*

Commitment

The C word, as it is called by many people who have an aversion to commitment, cannot be avoided. Individuals who are afraid of committing will find themselves committed to not committing or committed to avoiding commitment. One way or the other a commitment is made.

COACHING QUESTIONS: *What shows up for you when you consider making a commitment to a project, relationship or to anything? What stories, rationalizations or justifications arise that stop you from committing or following through with your commitment? Is it possible that you are honoring a commitment to your story, rationalization or justification? Are you willing to look at your relationship to commitment differently in order to empower yourself to actually have what it is you say you want?*

The Process of Making Commitments, Keeping Commitments and Breaking Commitments

By distinguishing these processes, you become more conscious of how you operate and notice more readily how you cause or allow interference with having what you say you want.

Commitments don't generally present themselves at a level of 100% yes or 100% no. There is the, "I'm committed enough now to make this declaration, put the money down and start the process." When the anxiety begins to show up—and anxiety always shows up—there will be a discernment process of figuring out if you are committed enough to take the next step.

Making Commitments

Something entices you into a relationship, project, job or a long-term purchase like a house, boat or car. You say yes and you are committed. Many of the commitments we make are based on wants and needs. I've been thinking I need a car in California so I have accessible transportation; my daughter decided she would sell her Cabriole for a car more suitable for the Colorado Rockies. Am I ready to make the commitment?

My wants, needs and values come into play when deciding to make a commitment. Questions arise of how does this fit into my financial picture. This car's emissions are higher than I would like. It won't be used much while I am gone. Would it be a waste of money? It's cute, sexy and sporty. Man! That would be fun to drive! Is it worth it? Each comment reflects various values that I support through my decisions.

COACHING QUESTIONS: *How do you make commitments? What is the thinking process through which you go that brings you to making the decision to commit or not to commit? What emotions and body sensations arise?*

Staying the Course of Commitment

COACHING QUESTIONS: *What has you stay in a commitment? What has you breaking a commitment? What beliefs do you have about commitments? What are you afraid people will find out or decide about you when you break commitments? What is your felt-sense, the quality of the experience in your body, when you break a commitment? What about when you stay in a commitment even though its value has worn thin—what's that like?*

There are people who jump out of commitments as quickly as they jump into them. Others will not break a commitment even though their lives may literally depend on it. In my mind, a commitment is like the life of an organism; it has a birth, middle and an end. Leaving prematurely could be a strategy for avoiding something: intimacy, anxiety, responsibility, many different things. Staying with a commitment long after its purpose has been lived out is also a strategy for avoiding something. Only you know what's true for you.

Much like knowing which values are driving your choice to make a commitment, it's knowing which ones have you staying in or breaking a commitment that is key.

Breaking a Commitment

Much like what happened with Frances, there is a time in every project when people begin to lose interest. The newness of the process begins to wear off; personality conflicts may begin to emerge; deadlines for papers and other required tasks begin to loom; the thought of actualizing your dream shifts from excitement and exhilaration to anxiety, fear and trepidation. The reality that, **"I'm going to have to start believing that I can have what I want"** looms large. All of the energy spent so far starts to weigh heavier, fear of success arises ever greater and the potential for creating failure increases. If you weren't feeling anxious before, you probably do now. Is this the time you begin to find ways to sabotage your success?

There are also those commitments into which we enter and over time, it becomes obvious that it is time to bring them to a finish.

COACHING QUESTIONS: *Have you had to end a relationship or a job when, perhaps others wanted you to stay? What was that like for you? How did you break the commitment? Is this the normal way you end commitments? To what degree would you say this is working for you? Would you consider seeing this another way if this wasn't working for you?*

There is no right, wrong, good or bad way to end a commitment; however, there are ways that could feel better than other ways. Have you known any couples who decided to end their marriage, but carry on their relationship through years of divorce proceedings? This is not an ending or a completion. Do you know people who decide to end their marriage and disappear completely never really finishing or completing with each other? These are strategies for avoiding vulnerability, intimacy and the grieving process that is essential in every ending.

Forever and for Always—No Matter What

In the series of Spiderman movies released in the past few years, we witness Spidey questioning his commitment to battling evil forces in service of protecting the innocent. He would like to settle down, and get married to Mary Jane, relax and drink a few brewskies over a baseball game. He isn't always 100% in alignment with his convictions. We've watched him quit and throw in the suit, but somehow, his conviction to have a good win over evil is rejuvenated and once again, he dons his suit and is on to the next opportunity to bring justice and harmony to the world.

There are times when the project or commitment is greater than you thought. Whenever we enter into a commitment, we never know what's going to show up.

Marlene and her husband Gary have struggled through a marriage commitment made many years ago. Gary suffered a massive stroke, at the age of 50 that left him paralyzed completely on the right side of his body. He had been a strong and athletic fellow who led eco-tours around the world. You can imagine what this did to Gary as a man who could no longer function in the world as he had. You can imagine what this did to their marriage; where there was a vital man, now lay a disabled being unable to be the partner he'd been once. You can imagine what this did to Marlene.

It's been 18 years of *being with* the consequences of that stroke and Marlene and Gary are still very much in love. Their commitment is forever and for always—no matter what!

When I heard about their commitment to each other, I was moved profoundly. Though I was 50 years old, I think it was the first time I truly understood what a deep and real commitment could look like. It gave me pause to consider how many of us move through our lives rarely being willing to put a stake in the ground and commit. Though they have their challenges, I envied the strength, courage and *conviction* that Gary and Marlene live into every day of their lives together.

Discipline

Discipline is easy if your level of commitment and your convictions are clear. It's not so easy when there is an underlying or conflicting commitment that wants to be served. When I think about finishing my Ph.D., it wasn't the enormity of academic brilliance that was required. It was the discipline to complete the *no-brainer* tasks that got it done. There were many hours spent making boxes in the form of graphs and tables, changing commas, doing very simple and mundane tasks. I thought, "This is so Mickey Mouse. How does this earn me a Ph.D.?" Of course, there was a ton of other aspects of this project that had me think and analyze data, integrate and synthesize information, but the bottom line to all of the tasks that had to be completed was my willingness *to do whatever it takes* to follow my conviction and my calling to complete a Ph.D. I didn't know where all of it would lead me. I just knew that I was curious enough to want to find out.

My client Deborah wants to lose 50 pounds before her fortieth birthday, which is nine months away. Though she says she is committed, she hasn't lost a pound in two and a half months. What needs to shift? She creates *excuses*, *rationalizations* and *justifications* for the fact that sometimes she just doesn't *feel* like going to the gym and doesn't *feel* like sticking to her diet. For Deborah, discipline would look like exercising those muscles that will get her to the gym, even when she doesn't *feel* like it and exercising the muscles that have her continue to eat according to her diet, even when she doesn't *feel* like it.

Many times, we give our power over to our feeling states, allowing them to make our decisions for us. Trust me on this one; your feelings will most often be the power drivers that will keep you from getting what you say you want. Feeling can be a specific strategy that supports you in continuing old patterns of relating to yourself, to others, and to your dreams. If these old patterns haven't worked for you in the past, they won't work for you now or in the future. Deborah will need to get intentional about the degree she is willing to actually succeed with her weight loss; otherwise, she and I are just wasting time and money while she creates another opportunity to disappoint herself.

Another client of mine wants me to be more of a spiritual teacher and less of a coach. What he really wants is someone to support him in staying safe in his very limited world of spiritual practice. He reads, meditates, prays and does yoga. He feels very successful in this realm. He lives in a blessed and *blessed-out* state a lot of the time. What's missing is that his creative urges are not being met beyond dabbling namby-pamby (a name he gave to that part of himself that isn't very interested in deepening the relationship with music and art). There isn't enough commitment or conviction yet to create any discipline. He also dabbles to avoid what might reveal itself if he was really committed to serving his creative urges. He has shared a number of times during our talks, "I don't know if I have what it takes. I think I lack confidence." At this time, he isn't ready to do whatever it takes.

Confidence

So many people walk around feeling un-empowered to go for what they want because they say they lack confidence. They believe they're missing something that, if it were present, would allow them to have what they say they want. What's missing?

COACHING QUESTIONS: *Close your eyes for just a second and imagine doing something that you are good at, something about which you feel confident. Search your internal database for all areas in your life where you feel confident. When and where did you feel most confident? What is the quality of that experience? What is the felt-sense of feeling confident?*

Most people who do this exercise experience five things: trust, self-love, clarity of intention, knowledge and experience. They feel they have *enough* knowledge, *enough* clarity of what they want, *enough* self-love and *enough* trust in themselves, in the world and in God (in whatever way they define God).

When people say they lack self-confidence, what they lack is one, some or all of the above and it's not an all or nothing proposition. It's that they lack *enough.* We live life on a continuum. We are rarely at one extreme or another. You've already experienced me asking questions such as, "On a scale from one to 100, to what degree are you…?" All of us can find where we are approximately on that continuum. In relation to confidence, each of us has some level of confidence. In one arena of your life, (let's say your career), you feel a great deal of confidence, but in another arena, perhaps in relationships, you have less confidence. Let's look at the aspects of confidence and see what your strong suits are.

Trust

COACHING QUESTIONS: *On a scale from zero to 100, to what degree do you trust yourself in relation to what you say you want? What would have to shift in order for that number to increase closer to 100 (i.e. if the number is 73, what would bring it up to 78 or 80)? Of what would you have to let go to experience more trust in yourself?*

If I lack enough trust in myself or in something greater than myself, I will withhold action. I will resist putting myself out into situations where something bad may happen. If I fail, I will be humiliated, embarrassed, isolated or rejected. I don't trust that I can handle failure and the humiliation or rejection that may follow. I don't trust people enough that I'll get the support I think I need. I only trust that they will criticize or make fun of me. What if I'm wrong about my ability to be successful in my life, relationships or career? What if I can't just do it? I don't trust God enough to give me what I want. He might punish me for wanting what I want.

Knowledge and Experience

If I think I lack **knowledge** and experience then I won't know enough and I will make mistakes. There is so much information out there and I've only studied for xx amounts of years and can't possibly know *enough* to be successful. How can I know enough? I'm new in this field and though I've studied and interned, I'm still not sure that I have what I need.

Clarity of Intention

What if what I think I want isn't what I want at all? How will I know if this is the right thing for me? What I want is different from what my parents want for me. My husband wants me to get a *real* job to help pay the bills. Why can't I be happy with just a simple career like everyone else? Why do I need to do something that has me move away from my home and friends? I want this job because it feels satisfying and meaningful, but the salary isn't sufficient. I don't know what to do.

Many people aren't willing to commit to anything because they are afraid that what they are committing to may not be it! This can actually be a strategy for avoiding risk and vulnerability, but they are also risking having a life. It can be challenging to get clear on what it is you want. Getting support for challenges like these would really work in your favor and this is some of the very work that coaches are trained to do.

Self-Love

I will sabotage any efforts to move forward towards that which I say I want to the degree that I lack self-love. I will act in ways that self-deprecates, supports failure and collapse and break down. I will direct myself into fields where I continue to harm myself by creating situations that make me feel bad, sad and mad. I'll invent conditions that support suffering, settling and surviving. I'll maintain my present beliefs that generate negativity, powerlessness and depression.

This whole book is about empowering you toward self-love, creating right-relationship with yourself and with that which you say you want. Distinguishing those strategies that have you avoid feeling good and loving from those strategies that support self-deprecating thoughts and beliefs will make a huge difference in how you show up for yourself and others. You will shift how you are being in the work, giving you greater capacity to create and manifest more fulfillment and satisfaction every day of your life.

Distinguishing the word confidence makes it easier to *be with* these specific aspects that can be confrontational. My experience is that by being with these aspects of confidence, you will uncover various conversations that inhibit your success. You'll also develop greater ease at entering into commitments, being in commitments and ending them when it is time.

****

The concepts we've covered in this chapter are all very challenging aspects of life, but without acknowledging our relationship to each one of them, we are acting from disabling beliefs and interpretations that won't get us where we say we want to go. Choosing to be responsible to the relationship we have to ourselves is foundational. What will it take you to step into your relationship with yourself intentionally?

My dad used to recite this poem from time to time. Of the many things he was, he was never a quitter.

Don't Quit

When things go wrong, as they sometimes will,
When the road you're trudging seems all uphill,
When the funds are low and the debts are high,
And you want to smile, but you have to sigh,
When care is pressing you down a bit,
Rest if you must, but don't you quit.

Life is queer with its twists and turns,
As every one of us sometimes learns.
And many a failure turns about,
When he might have won had he stuck it out.
Don't give up though the pace seems slow.
You may succeed with another blow.

Success is failure turned inside out,
The silver tint of the clouds of doubt,
And you never can tell how close you are,
It may be near when it seems so far.
So stick to the fight when you're hardest hit.
It's when things seem worst
That you must not quit.

~Author Unknown

Practice Areas

- If you've answered the coaching questions in this chapter, you've done a great deal of work already. No practice areas for you! Just acknowledge the courage it takes to be present and committed enough to do the work.
- If you haven't done the coaching questions, I encourage you to go back and do them. You can't help, but shift something, even if you just read them. See what happens.

Chapter 7: The Wisdom of No Escape

"I'm not afraid of storms, for I'm learning how to sail my ship."
Louisa May Alcott, *Little Women*

What Have I Got to Lose

If I had been able to get off that sailboat in the middle of the Atlantic Ocean, I would have. It was too damn scary for me day after day and mind you, it was only three weeks – 21 days. Millions of people on this planet have much worse conditions where they survive for years on end, but for me, I had escaped from that experience. I would have stepped out of one of the most profound and at the same time, humbling experiences life had ever thrown at me. I would have missed deepening my trust in Spirit, in this boat that was created for such an adventure. I would have missed the opportunity to find a far more powerful *me* than I ever thought I would discover. I would have missed the opportunity to stand in dignity and grace amidst human calamity.

I stepped off the boat, *Tree of Life*, for the last time in Portugal, and headed back to the United States to find what was next for me. I never regretted the experience on that adventure and I am so grateful for where it brought me, to this moment with you.

The Wisdom of No Escape

There is something sacred that occurs when things don't go the way you want; some mystical and ineffable event transpires. The twist of events that created this *be with*—whatever *this* is—supports an awakening to wisdom not realized prior to this present and challenging condition. As long as you are alive, you are susceptible to every human predicament and suffering known to man and woman. None of us knows if or when we will be hit with a major catastrophe, but it is inevitable that something will happen and you won't like it. That's the bad news. The good news is that in the end, you will be extremely grateful for the opportunity to *be with* yourself through the process. Through this experience, you will have developed maturity, wisdom and most importantly, a greater knowing of your capacity to *be with* whatever comes your way. Power and success will mean something different to you then. Showing up in integrity and accountability will feel essential and gratifying in ways you never thought possible.

Stop the World—I Want to Get Off

There will be times; however, when no matter how powerful you've become and no matter what skills you have developed to be successful, accountable and in integrity, life will feel hopeless and you will be powerless to do anything about it. It will be impossible to shift the circumstances and consequences to be in your favor. In these times, you will be miserable. You will hurt and be uncomfortable by physical manifestations of whatever is troubling you. Emotions will surge and you won't know exactly what you're feeling. There's nowhere to run and nowhere to hide. During these moments, it's just a big-fat-*be-with.*

A big-fat-*be-with* is what shows up when there's nothing to do, but be with your circumstances and witness how they are separate from you. It's comparable to being on a sailboat a thousand miles from nowhere and there is no escape. You have to *be with* the unsettling effect with no control over the situation; however, you have the resilience and wisdom to be in your big-fat-*be-with* in a way that may minimize suffering and anguish. It gives you the capacity to view your situation from a different vantage point, consciously taking yourself outside the discomfort, pain and suffering in order to experience the whole event from a larger perspective.

COACHING QUESTIONS: *What is the quality of the experience of being in a situation where you have no control? How do you* be with *yourself during those times? What strategies do you use to avoid or distract yourself from being with the consequences of your present circumstances? What's possible during these times when you feel hopeless and powerless?*

Developing self-knowledge through life experiences is in itself, self-empowering. As you go through life, especially if you can be conscious of how you *be,* you develop a different perspective. This new perspective creates new possibilities for choosing to see yourself differently, to see that perhaps, your perceived limitations were unfounded. Amazing experiences will test your willingness forever and your capacity to be with events, circumstances and consequences of your *being* and actions, in service to you surviving and perhaps more importantly, in service to you *thriving.*

It doesn't serve you to feel the anxiety that accompanies your worries of what might happen to you in the midst of the turbulence of any circumstance: an airplane ride or the death of a dream, but anxiety is inevitable. Anxiety is a messenger that says, "STOP! GO NO FURTHER! YOU ARE ENTERING DANGEROUS TERRITORY!" Anxiety is a primal response to warn us of the dangers that lay beyond the confines of our tribal territory. We will live forever into the unknown. Anxiety will always accompany us on our journey. How we *be* with our anxiety of the unknown is changing as we discover our personal power to *be with what is.* Though there are prophecies of doom and gloom and prophecies of greater global peace and awakening, we have no idea what is unfolding. We have no control over the future. We have control only over how we *be* and how we choose to *be with* what is now.

As I write this, there is an ambulance siren in the distance. Someone is in physical trouble and most likely unanticipated trouble. I imagine the people involved are distressed and anxious. What will happen next? They have to *be with* the circumstances, anxiety, worry, suffering and the unknown. What will hold them together in times like these? How will they handle the outcome? Self-empowerment contributes to the well-being of everyone involved and allows each of them to move to a larger capacity to *be with* what they thought they couldn't be with. I truly believe that, if you haven't yet created opportunities to expand your capacity for self-empowerment, you will create them through episodes, such as the one facing the individual who needed the ambulance. There is no escaping the *be with* of our human drama.

COACHING QUESTIONS: *When you can't escape your environment or your circumstances, what will you do? What do you do when there is nothing to do? What shows up in the midst of being* with what is?

While being with yourself, which in fact is all you can be because you have no other choice; otherwise, you will lose your mind; things happen that will reveal stuff to you. You begin to see the gifts within the hopelessness and powerlessness. You find what is beyond your thinking and your beliefs. Do you remember the bumper sticker I mentioned earlier? "DON'T ALWAYS BELIEVE WHAT YOU THINK!" If you haven't noticed already, you have been given numerous opportunities to see things differently. You've decided to think and to believe what you believe and think. My experience is that those thoughts and beliefs can change in a blink of an ambulance siren, a diagnosis of cancer, a zero balance in your checkbook, the love of your life walking out the door, a raise in pay, the sound of a newborn baby breathing…

Change

Change is inevitable. We have *no choice;* we grow and mature. In those ways, change is happening to us, and then there is change that we can control. This sort of change occurs mostly in the *doing* of life. You may change the way you eat, dress, drive your car, or you may change what you believe or the way you think about things. Generally, change takes place within a specific context of your life. You, in your essential being, may not change, but change only the things you *do.*

Ron Heifetz, a Harvard professor says it is not change itself that disturbs people; it is the loss that accompanies change. With change, stability is lost; relationship to one's perceived reality and identity as we knew it can disappear. Who you are now, after having read this book, is different than who you were prior to opening these pages. You can't *not* be affected by what you invite into your reality.

There is madness to being in this world, facing reality every day, to find only that what you had perceived once as real wasn't real at all. You made it up to support and validate the tribal chords—your family or community's beliefs—those that they made up too. Trying to stay within the confines of the semblance of a reality that no longer exists for you is impossible, just as it would be madness to try and remain enthralled with a magician's magic once you known how the trick is done. Change happens to us *and* change happens through choice.

COACHING QUESTIONS: *What do you do when faced with different views of reality? Do you deny, ignore, avoid, discount or reject? How does denying, ignoring, etc. serve self-empowerment for you? What values are served through these specific strategies? What, if anything, is being avoided or denied?*

My point here is that, if you are not *open* to change, you will be *opened* to change through circumstances and events that appear beyond your control. I've heard an expression somewhere similar to the wisdom of no escape. It's the wisdom of the two-by-four. If we don't empower ourselves to wake up and be conscious of our truth, integrity and accountability for how our lives unfold, the two-by-four appears magically to do the job.

Transcendence

Sometimes you see how the trick is done, but then forget. Sometimes you see beyond the veils of illusion and have great epiphanies; realizations about yourself and the world that feels like it will change everything forever; however, sometimes these moments of transcendence are forgotten and you return to the comfort of the *what is,* as you have always known it to be.

So many of us, especially those of us born and raised in a Western culture are not familiar with the concept of transcendence, except where it pertains to Jesus and other Biblical characters whose lives were transformed by miracles and other mystical experiences. Eastern religions and philosophies promote transcendence of every human being. These transcending moments contribute to an awakening of our consciousness that allows an expanded sense of presence while on this earthly plain. Of what good is this expanded, conscious presence? What does it serve?

COACHING QUESTIONS: *Let's say that you are 37 years old. You've had a good enough life, some interesting relationships that support your sense of well-being. Let's give you an opportunity to go back to when you were seven years old, erasing what you have learned and experienced for the past thirty years. From the vantage point of a seven-year-old, what does life look like? What is possible from a seven-year-old child's perspective? Did you have a clue of what your life would look like, even a few years down the road? Did you know that in 30 years your life would look and feel as it does now? What did you want when you were seven?*

Coming back to being 37: What experiences have you had that supported you being who you are now? What beliefs and interpretations have you transcended about yourself, other people or the world that has allowed you to reach this present level of success financially, emotionally or spiritually? What two-by-fours came along to support you moving towards who you are now? Are you presently requiring any new two-by-fours to support you in where you want to go? What practices and changes can you take on to support getting what you say you want?

Transformation

Transformation is different from change and transcendence. Transformation is sustained transcendence. Events and realizations that have created changes in the way you *be* in the world are transformative in nature, as opposed to change that takes place more by doing. With transformation, the knowledge you've gained and the level of awakening to which you have come, will be with you always. You won't go back to sleep; no matter how hard you try.

Most people say they want transformation. They want the magical mystery thing to happen so they can have their dream-life come true. I've been working in the field of transformation for a very long time and the fact is there is a great deal of responsibility that comes along with transformation. Being enlightened doesn't mean that life doesn't get bumpy or there aren't challenging decisions to be with or that money or relationships are effortless. Transformation, in my experience, is like moving from junior high school to senior high school. You can only guess what it's like, but you haven't a clue until you are there.

I facilitated a women's retreat in Colorado last weekend. Eighteen women from all over the country convened in the mountains, most of them strangers to each other, to me and to the process of transformation. They were all there to experience something in order to be transformed and have a better life. Their wish came true, at least in that they each had an experience that opened their eyes to ways they were *being* that will never allow them to fall back to sleep in the same way.

They each went back to their lives as prepared as they could be to live more fully from this awakened state, but in our last couple of hours together, when we explored what support they might want in order to continue to move forward in their desire for a better life, what surfaced was anxiety and worry. "How do I *be* this, in the face of a husband who is distant and unavailable?" "My life doesn't allow me to maintain this level of personal presence." "I'd have to find new friends who would actually support me in being open, alive and true to myself." "I would have to quit my job and find work that nourishes my soul, something that is fun and fulfilling." "People will think I'm weird if I'm this happy and kind." Each of these women will consciously face the dilemma of how she will *be with* the circumstances of her life. She may decide to put the blinders back on and the earplugs back in. She would work at forgetting the experience of transformation in order to maintain her present reality, or she could decide to be different, expose the charade of her way of being up until now and work with the others to support the transformative process to further self-expression, in the most authentic sense. Each woman will empower herself to the degree in which she is prepared and willing to risk annihilation of her false-self and begin to assume real responsibility that comes with truly authoring one's self and one's life.

The Personal Is the Political

Carol Gilligan, author of *In a Different Voice,* states that the personal is the political

The responsibility of claiming your life, empowering yourself to live responsibly to others and within yourself means that you begin to take a stand for your own truth and you make meaning based on your perceptions and truth and not anyone else's.

I've never considered myself political in any way. In fact, I have always hated politics. I hate the deception, the lack of accountability and integrity that seems tied to politics. I got that by being who I am and how I am *being*; I am making a political statement. I came to understand this by reading some of Carol Gilligan's work in, *In a Different Voice* and her statement that the personal *is* political. I began to see that I'm *being* a declaration for what is true for me.

In my adolescence and most of my adulthood, I stood in righteous indignation toward the inept parenting I received. I also was taking a stand for being feminine and inept as I could be to get someone to take care of me. I took many stands, most of which didn't get much support or change and were never truly empowering; nonetheless, each stand I took stood as a political statement. Again, I didn't set out to be political. I just set out to try to be me and would try to be recognized for what I wanted to bring to the table.

My truths about being a woman and a human being have changed immensely over the decades and I acknowledge now that what I wanted was to avoid a life filled with pain and disappointment. I practiced strategies that I thought would keep me risk-free. Well, I've made it clear hopefully that, that isn't a realistic perspective on life. Through the process of taking responsibility for how my life is showing up, I'm now able to take a stand consciously for a life worth living.

Now my beliefs are that, through a self-empowering relationship with life, transformation and awakening happens. The responsibility that comes with this process is accepted and stepped into consciously. There is a realization that personal truth is worth taking a stand. Like many of the women at the Colorado retreat who were returning home to family, friends and their jobs, they were going to have to decide to what degree they were committed to being true to their essential selves and true to the other women who witnessed their unveiling and discovering. They will be with this dilemma as all of us are. When we reveal a truth bigger than the lie we've been living, how shall we live?

Dignity: Is It Worth It

I had a transformational experience once when I caught the last few moments of a movie on television. It changed my life. The last scene was of an African-American man and his granddaughter walking down a sidewalk with their backs straight and their heads held high. There was something that I wanted, and that they had; they had dignity.

When I am unsure how to define some elusive concept, I go inside, check in with my body and inquire, "What's the quality of the experience?" Dignity is a very challenging concept to define and yet we all have a sense of what it is. My body's sensations tell me that dignity goes beyond egoic-pride, courage and self-esteem. It's more in alignment with concepts like self-worth, self-respect, self-authorship, fearless self-expression and clarity of my value in just being me.

The quality of pride is not arrogance. There is knowing, beyond certainty and beyond any doubt that there is a sense that I am loved unconditionally, just as I am. I may have faults, but I am not flawed in my being. I experience self-love from this place. I have nothing to hide and nothing to gain from pretense and arrogance, pridefulness or self-importance. I have nothing to lose by being me. Grace, not disgrace. I don't have to manage myself to meet others' standards or my own perceptions of what others expect of me. I cannot be threatened. Only my managed egoic-self can be threatened. When my illusional self crumbles, what's left is me!

I require strategies no longer to protect or defend. I practice living without pretense that means, owning my mistakes and failures without rationalizing or justifying. All of the shame and indignity that encumbered me for decades falls away. Any disgraceful experiences are forgotten in the light of compassion, which at this moment, flows through in brilliant and radiant light. I'm now standing for this way of *being* and I am willing to stand in the political as well.

What's at Stake

Many of my clients' stories have been left in mid-air. Each one of them continues to meet the next choice-point. They will choose again to leap into a new belief, a new way of being and a new action to support their desired outcome, or not. Their challenges and desires for a more fulfilling life will never cease. Their destiny, like yours and mine, is to expand and live into the potential of their lives. The will come to choice-points constantly and navigate the new *be-withs* of those moments. There are no *happily-ever-afters*. There is only, I believe, happier, more fulfilling and more meaningful ever-afters.

Whoever you are, wherever you are in your development, what is absolutely true is that you have shown up as real as you can and you know it. Even with all of your personas, façades, strategies and manipulations, you are expressing yourself as completely as is possible in this present moment. You can feel on track with that and you have the mechanism inside that empowers you to navigate. It's what got you here. It's what will get you to what's next. This compass steers you toward your destiny; empowered fully to meet yourself as you never thought possible.

There will be times in your life when many of the strategies shared in this book will be useful. The personal power that you've exercised and strengthened gives you what you need to be with whatever comes your way. It doesn't mean you can fix it, heal it or make it go away. You still wouldn't be able to step off a boat onto the safety of the shore while in the middle of the ocean; however, it does give you the resilience and wisdom to be in your life in a way that may minimize suffering and anguish of your present circumstances. It gives you the capacity to view your situation from a different vantage point, taking yourself consciously outside the discomfort, pain and suffering in order to experience the whole event from a larger perspective.

****

Bree, a brilliant and up-and-coming leadership coach had a profound realization the other day. As she was envisioning the work into which she is stepping, she realized that her vision evolved around self-empowerment as the vehicle of collective and collaborative leadership that leads to global change. She realized that the key to bringing peace and compassion to the world was through this process of self-empowerment. She also realized that as she steps into right-relationship with herself, she is far more compassionate to herself. As this compassion deepens, her capacity for compassion toward others grows by leaps and bounds. She got it that she is a living experiment of creating peace and compassion on Earth. Global change no longer felt out of reach for Bree and self-empowerment now meant that transformation of one is transformation for everyone.

Practice Areas

- Make a list of what, if anything was valuable for you in these chapters. What made you stop and think? How do you want to take this to the next level? To what are you willing to commit?
- Where in your life have you experienced soulful satisfaction? In what ways would you like to bring more of this experience into your life?
- What is the feeling of ultimate integrity?
- What is your experience of dignity?
- What would need to shift in order for more dignity, integrity and soulful satisfaction to be present?
- Practice experiencing dignity. Experience the felt-sense of dignity in your body. Create more opportunities to bring these qualities of dignity into your life as often as you can. Write about your experience.
- Acknowledge yourself for your curiosity and fascination with your life enough to read this book and perhaps do the practice areas and coaching questions.
- Acknowledge all the amazing ways that you have been *being* that have brought you to this moment in your life. Celebrate your success and know that these are the foundations upon which you are building the rest of your life.

A Final Story: Nasreddin Hodja and the Donkeys

Once upon a time Nasreddin Hodja, the famous trickster, was walking toward the border between his country and another. He led a donkey by a rope, and the donkey was laden with straw.

When the border inspector spied Hodja, he smiled and rubbed his hands gleefully. "Ah, this man is a trickster, and surely he is smuggling something. Watch this," he whispered to his fellow inspectors. "I shall find his smuggled goods."

The inspector stopped Hodja. "Sir, you must allow me to search your donkey. I am certain you are attempting to smuggle valuable goods across the border into Persia."

Hodja nodded solemnly. "Search away, good fellow," he said, "but I'm afraid you'll find nothing, but straw."

The inspector frowned. "Everyone knows you're a trickster," he said, "and that you always have a trick up your sleeve."

Hodja nodded again, and the inspector began his search. He pulled at the bundles of straw, scattering straw here, there and everywhere. He reached inside each bundle. He called to his assistants and they examined the straw bundles carefully.

But search as they would, the inspectors found nothing hidden in Hodja's straw, and so they sent him on his way across the border.

A week later Hodja returned, once again leading a donkey laden with straw. "Ah ha," the inspector said to him, "you likely think we won't search you this time, but you are wrong."

The inspector called to every assistant, and 10 men plucked and pulled and yanked at the straw, tossing it everywhere and making quite a mess.

But the men found nothing at all, and the inspector had no choice, but to let Hodja pass the border.

The next week the same thing happened, and the same happened the next. Every week for many months, Hodja led his donkey to the border, and every week for many months, the inspector eyed him with the greatest suspicion. As time passed, the inspector's determination to expose Hodja as a smuggler grew fiercer, and every week his searches took longer.

Still Hodja never lost his temper nor grew upset. He simply stood and waited while the search went on, and every single time, the inspectors found no hidden treasure.

A year passed this way. Word spread far and wide. "The border patrol believe Hodja's a smuggler," people said, but no one could prove this was true.

However, the rumors persisted. People wondered what he might be smuggling. Did he carry valuable coins across the border? Was he hiding gold, perhaps? Or maybe he transformed the straw itself into gold, as some said magicians could do. Could Hodja be more than a trickster? Perhaps he was a magician too.

In this way, Hodja's reputation as a clever smuggler spread far and wide, across every border.

Still the inspector was determined to undo the plump little man with the unfailingly serene expression. "No one will outwit me," he promised, and so each time Hodja appeared, the inspector searched his donkey and straw.

This went on for years. The inspector grew old, and soon it was time for him to retire. "I cannot stop working until I have discovered Hodja's secret," he swore, and so he worked on, well past retirement age, deep into old age.

At long last he was far too tired to go to work, and his eyesight was failing. Finally, he left his post.

But he never stopped thinking of Hodja. Had he smuggled treasures in the donkey's tail? Perhaps they should have searched the donkey's mouth. He sent word to the border men, and so they continued to search.

And then one day Hodja simply stopped crossing the border.

Still the inspector could not stop thinking of him. He decided to visit Hodja in his hometown of Aksehir, for he realized that he would never be satisfied until he had gotten the truth out of him. So, he traveled across the border.

He found Hodja sitting idly in the marketplace, enjoying the warmth of the sun and the sweetness of his coffee. "Sir," said the inspector, "excuse me, but I have to know. I cannot rest. All those years you crossed the border and we searched you; surely you were smuggling something."

Hodja looked at the inspector and smiled his warmest smile. Slowly he nodded.

"Please, you must tell me. What was it? Gold? Silver? Were you smuggling food or spirits? Cloth, perhaps? Where did you hide it?"

With each guess Hodja just shook his head.

"Won't you tell an old man, sir? I'll never rest in peace unless I know."

And because Hodja was a kind man and did not wish the inspector to spend the rest of his days worrying, he nodded, "Yes, I'll tell you now. I was smuggling donkeys."

****

During my studies at the Institute of Transpersonal Psychology, two of my favorite classes offered were in Sufism. That is where I met Nasreddin and his donkeys. It was there that I learned, at least within teaching, smuggling donkeys became a metaphor for smuggling spiritual teachings and transformation.

Suggested Reading

Arntz, William, Chasse, Betsy & Vicente, Mark (2005). *What the Bleep Do We Know!?: Discovering the Endless Possibilities for Altering your Everyday Reality.* Deerfield Beach, FL: Health Communications.

Bach, Richard (1997). *Illusions: The Adventures of a Reluctant Messiah.* New York: Delacorte.

Braden, Greg (1997). *Walking Between the Worlds: The Science of Compassion.* Bellevue, WA: Radio Bookstore Press.

Buchholz, Quint. "Giacomond." www.artprints.com.

Campbell, Susan (2001). *Getting Real.* Tiburon, CA: Kramer Books.

Carlson, Richard (2007). *Don't Sweat the Small Stuff...and it's all small stuff: Simple Ways to Keep the Little Things from Taking Over Your Life.* New York: MJF Books/Fine Communications.

Carnes, Patrick (1993). *A Gentle Path through the Twelve Steps: The Classic Guide for All People in the Process of Recovery.* Center City, MN: Hazelden.

Covey, Stephen (1989). *The 7 Habits of Highly Effective People.* New York: Simon and Schuster.

Flaherty, James J. (1998). *Coaching: Evoking Excellence in Others.* Newton, MA: Butterworth-Heinemann.

Fromm, Erich (1976). *To Have or To Be?* New York: Harper & Row.

Gendlin, Eugene (1978). *Focusing.* New York: Everest House.

Gilligan, Carol (1993). *In a Different Voice: Psychological Theory and Women's Development.* Cambridge, MA: Harvard University Press.

Goss, Tracy (1996). *The Last Word on Power: Reinvention for Leaders and Anyone Who Must Make the Impossible Happen.* New York: Doubleday.

Grabhorn, Lynn (2000). *Excuse Me, Your Life is Waiting: The Astonishing Power of Feeling*. Charlottesville, VA: Hampton Roads Publishing Company.

Grof, Stan (1988). *The Adventures of Self-Discovery: Dimensions of Consciousness and New Perspectives in Psychotherapy and Inner Exploration.* Albany, NY: SUNY.

Hawkins, David R. (2002). *Power vs. Force: The Hidden Determinants of Human Behavior*. Carlsbad, CA: Hay House, Inc.

Hicks, Esther and Jerry (2004). *Ask and It Is Given: Learning to Manifest Your Desires*. Carlsbad, CA: Hay House, Inc.

Hicks, Esther and Jerry (2006). *The Amazing Power of Deliberate Intent: Living the Art of Allowing*. Carlsbad, CA: Hay House, Inc.

Jeffers, Susan (1987). *Feel the Fear and Do It Anyway*. New York: Ballentine Books.

Levine, Stephen (1982). *Who Dies?* New York: Anchor Books/Doubleday.

Lipton, Bruce (2005). *The Biology of Belief: unleashing the power of consciousness, matter & Miracles*. Santa Rosa, CA: Mountain of Love/Elite Books.

McCombs, Chris (2007). *Apprenticeship of the Soul: Wisdom of Sonjan.* Unpublished. (Author of Delicious Silence and The Beloved.)

McKenna, Jed (2004). *Spiritually Incorrect Enlightenment*. Iowa City, IA: Wisefool Press.

Maisel, Eric (1995). *Fearless Creating*. New York: Tarcher/Putnam.

Maisel, Eric (2005). *Coaching the Artist Within*. Novato, CA: New World Library.

Maisel, Eric (2007). *Creativity for Life*. Novato, CA: New World Library.

Maisel, Eric (2007). *Ten Zen Seconds*. Napperville, IL: Sourcebooks.

Obissier, Patrick (2006). *Biogeneology: Decoding the Psychic Roots of Illness.* Rochester, VT: Inner Transitions International/The Healing Arts Press.

Parks, Sharon Daloz (2005). *Leadership Can Be Taught: A Bold Approach for a Complex World.* Boston: Harvard Business School Press.

Rasha (2002). *Oneness/Channeled by Rasha.* San Diego, CA: Jodere Group.

Rinpoche, Sogyal (1992). *The Tibetan Book of Living and Dying.* New York: HarperCollins.

Dr. Seuss (1990). *Oh, the Places You'll Go!* New York: Random House.

Sieler, Alan (2003). *Coaching to the Human Soul: Ontological Coaching and Deep Change.* Australia: Publishing Solution.

Sinetar, Marsha (1987). *Do What You Love, the Money Will Follow.* New York: Dell.

Tolle, Eckhart (1999). *The Power of Now.* Novato, CA: New World Library.

Acknowledgements

For many years, I experienced writing as a solitary endeavor a time of creativity, when the concepts wanting to be explored needed quiet, uninhibited expression to birth themselves. I sequestered myself a great deal to allow the process to unfold, but about eight months ago, more and more I needed people with which to confer regarding, well, regarding every aspect of writing. This project became a collaborative venture with many hearts and minds. I am so grateful to have been given the gift of friendship and love from all of you who have supported the birthing of this book and of me in this present version of done.

I'd like to acknowledge a few people who've empowered me and this project to its completion:

Todd Zimmerman, my sweetie —You've walked this road with me for many years. You graciously share your wisdom and mastery of the coaching process and your expertise of humanity to deepen what is revealed in these pages. You knew how to take a concept and bring in more meaning, more richness, texture and depth. Your support and encouragement inspired me.

Todd Phillips—My friend and Life Coach, I acknowledge you for your passionate and heart-centered approach. You creatively contoured the process to bring me to my work as a mid-wife of this book. You created a container within which I untied the knots holding me hostage to something less than a full capacity to finish this project.

Fabian Espinoza—I am always in awe of the creations that come through you. You captured the essence of this book through image and color. I felt like a small child awaiting Christmas morning to open the wrappings of your designs. Like you, they are magical and inspiring.

Eric Maisel, Creativity Coach Extraordinaire—I acknowledge you for the gift of your time, your support and your presence as I practice this art of writing. I so appreciate your readiness to answer questions that kept me moving forward with the countless aspects of writing that needed attention.

Noah and Hannah—You are living examples of self-empowerment. I have such respect for you and for your courage to create your lives according to your blueprints. Though it appears at times challenging and curious, from a parent's perspective, your visions keep you on your own path and your heart's desire beckons the world to your door.

Margaret Hartwell and Magdalen Bowyer, my Writing Coaches & Sydney Reuben, Beverly Blackwell, Pat Hall and Laura Snider, My Readers—I acknowledge you all for your friendship and support and for the time you've given to read these chapters many times over. Your brilliance shines through all of these pages.

My Clients, Students and Trainees—You have been my real teachers. Through our hours, weeks, months and years together, I have been honored to experience the miracle of birth a million times over. You've allowed me to witness and learn so much from you, the culmination being what's showing up on these pages. You are transforming the world, and in so many ways, are my lifeline to the Divine.

The Institute of Transpersonal Psychology—You have been the container within which I've cooked for over a decade. You've given me the space to grow as a student into a mentor/supervisor, into faculty and facilitator. You have given me the gift of belief and trust in my vision and my truth. You encourage expression outside the box for every individual with the belief that this is the way to bring forth a more loving, compassionate and fulfilling way of being on this planet. I acknowledge, more specifically, Dr. Robert Frager, Dr. Jim Fadiman, Dr. Arthur Hastings and Dr. Paul Roy. Each of you holds the light and the heart for us to see and know who we really are.

Hans Phillips—You appeared in my life magically and turned it upside down. You brought clarity to the muddy waters. Your coaching, training program and loving, blessed heart allowed collaborative projects to be birthed and find their own way. There are few days that go by that you do not come to mind. I feel a profound gratitude for all the gifts you've given to me and to the world.

Gloria Taylor—You were my first real spiritual teacher. Through the process of learning to be a Marriage and Family Therapist, and through therapy, mentoring, supervision and friendship, I awakened to a deeper knowing of the capacity to be real and to love myself and to love humanity. Through my relationship with you, I learned to listen beyond words, to that which forms the words, to that which is beyond the words, to that which is the spirit and the soul's essence of every living being. I believe you saved my life in so many ways. I believe too that you touch the lives of every client and every student, every relationship I attend to. Though our contacts have been very brief since we worked together 25 years ago, you are still a magnificent presence in my life.

Mark Brady—I acknowledge you for being the seed of inspiration for beginning this book. Your charismatic presence lightened my way and showed how effortless this process can be. Not that you ever knew it, but you more than anyone held me accountable to my commitment to finish this book. It's funny, we never know the impact we have on each other's lives.

Last, but definitely not least, I acknowledge Creation itself. The Great Mystery, God, Goddess, Universal Oneness, Source of all that is. It is You, it is Us that breathes life into every being. I am grateful for the way that it is.

Dr. Rosie Kuhn is the founder of the Paradigm Shifts Coaching Group, author of Self-Empowerment 101 and creator and facilitator of the Transformational Coaching Training Program. She is a Life, Spiritual and Business Coach to individuals, corporations and executives, known for empowering her clients in making rapid, transformational changes to their lives and relationships. She lives on beautiful Orcas Island where she runs Wonderful Women's Retreats every summer.

Please visit her website and discover how Dr. Rosie can impact your life in ways you may never have thought possible. http://dr-rosie.com.

CPSIA information can be obtained at www.ICGtesting.com
Printed in the USA
LVOW090749100812
293632LV00003B/333/P